THE ORIGIN OF CHINESE CHARACTERS

THE ORIGIN OF CHINESE CHARACTERS

AN ILLUSTRATED HISTORY AND WORD GUIDE

KIHOON LEE

Algora Publishing
New York

Library of Congress Cataloging-in-Publication Data —

Names: Lee, Kihoon, 1972- author.
Title: The origin of chinese characters: an illustrated history and word
    guide / Kihoon Le.
Description: New York: Algora Publishing, 2018.
Identifiers: LCCN 2018009601 (print) | LCCN 2018015460 (ebook) | ISBN
    9781628943238 (pdf) | ISBN 9781628943214 (soft cover: alk. paper) | ISBN
    9781628943221 (hard cover: alk. paper)
Subjects: LCSH: Chinese characters—History. | Chinese language—Etymology.
Classification: LCC PL1171 (ebook) | LCC PL1171 .L335 2018 (print) | DDC
    495.11/1—dc23
LC record available at https://lccn.loc.gov/2018009601

Printed in the United States

Table of Contents

Introduction

In ancient times in China, people believed that they could tell fortunes by grilling a tortoise shell, a turtle shell or an ox's shoulder blade over the fire. When the heat expanded the cracks in this "oracle bone," the pattern would be interpreted, and the results of such pyromantic divinations were etched on the surface with a sharp iron instrument.

Such writings or characters are called "Jia-Gu Characters"; the name of "Jia-Gu" was formed by taking each character from Tortoise Shell (Jia) and Cow Bone (Gu). Excavations near Anyang (Henan Province) have turned up huge troves of such carvings, tens of thousands of them, since the 1920s. These sacred characters were made by Shang Dynasty people (1600–1046 BC) who used to live near the HuangHe (Yellow River) area.

Tortoise Plastron with Divination Inscription (Jia) and Scapula Bone with Inscription (Gu) (16ʰ-11ʰ century BC) <National Museum of China>

Kings or shamans believed they could consult the gods, through fortune telling, about all affairs of the state, and so they sought guidance regarding political and military events, economics and ceremonial needs. These writings tell the results of the fortune or prophecies told by gods.

The most important of the gods was Shang Di (上帝), the god of Heaven.

Sculpture of a Shang Dynasty Man (13ᵗʰ century-11ᵗʰ century BC) <Yinxu Museum>

After the fall of the dynasty, the people scattered. China's prestigious ancient history books record that at least one faction migrated to Joseon (ancient Korea, 2333–108 BC).

In fact, the Shang Dynasty that invented these Chinese characters had many customs in common with ancient Korea, and even today many of the customs of the Shang Dynasty remain in use. Koreans place great value on the color white, they pay respect on their knees or bow at the waist when they express their respect to others. Thus when analyzing ancient Chinese characters, we can find many similarities between ancient China and current Korea.

The new residents who defeated the Shang Dynasty also contributed to building the characters. The shapes of the Chinese characters changed gradually and became more sophisticated. After several typographical changes, about 1800 years ago, the Han Dynasty people elaborated the Chinese characters and they came to look like the ones used now; the characters were called Hanzi (The Characters of Han). The Hanzi (set of Chinese Characters) is beautiful from both the typographic and artistic viewpoints.

The people of Han Dynasty (AD 25-220) <National Museum of China>

Since then, the Hanzi characters remained mostly the same and were used in East Asia for over 2000 years. However, due to historical and cultural changes, few people remember the original history and meanings of the characters. Scholars have had to approach this like a code, and it has been a great challenge to break the etymology and history behind some Hanzi characters.

In this book, I reflect and agree with the etymology theories of Hanzi written by current scholars, but I also attempt to propose my own analysis and interpretations as well.

The Chinese characters in this book are mostly essential characters that are widely used in contemporary China. Readers of this book may learn many key Chinese characters with the explanation of their origins and may gain a deeper understanding of not only the Chinese, but also of the Japanese and the Korean cultures, who received so much influence from China in ancient times.

Bird-shaped pottery pot. The ancient Chinese worshiped birds, because they could fly close to Heaven, the most worshiped God. (Neolithic Age) <National Museum of China>

In mainland China, some of the more complicated characters were simplified in the mid-20th century. Therefore each character in this book will be explained in the order below:

(1) Traditional Chinese Character
(2) Simplified Chinese Character
(3) Pronunciation (Pinyin = Wade-Giles)
(4) Meaning

For example,

      (1) 鄉
      (2) 乡
      (3) xiang=hsiang
      (4) countryside

PART 1 天
(TIAN=T'IEN) HEAVEN

1. THE GOD OF HEAVEN

East Asian philosophy starts with "One"

Before the invention of Hanzi (Chinese characters), the Chinese used knots (rope) or simple symbols. As the society became more complex, the need for more efficient ways for communication were needed. Hanzi (Chinese characters) were developed to meet such needs.

What did the early writers think to express number "one"? As children use their fingers to count, the ancient people used twigs and sticks to express numbers and to count.

A twig ‾ (一, yi, one), two twigs = (二, er, two), three twings ≡ (三, san, three) four twigs ≣ (四, si=ssu, four) became the letters from 1 to 4.

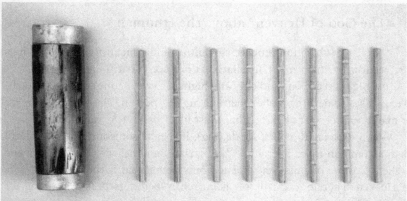

Branches used for telling fortunes or for calculation (14ᵗʰ-19ᵗʰ century) <National Museum of Korea >

However, "one" 一 (yi, one) does not simply mean the number one in the numerical sense.

In AD 100, a Chinese scholar wrote a book "Shuo Wen Jie Zi" which provides many explanations behind Hanzi. Among over 9,000 Hanzi characters in this book, the "one (一)" is explained first as followed:

> "In the beginning there was only One Way, and this Way divided earth from heaven and made everything."

As we can see, "one" is not just a simple tree twig. It is also philosophically understood as the "sole principle" from which heaven, earth and living things originate d from.

Jade Dragon and Phoenix (10,000-4,000 years ago): The dragon and the phoenix had been taken as the emblems of Chinese civilization. <Liaoning Provincial Museum>

"The God of Heaven" above the Hhuman

一 (一, yi, One) influenced its philosophical meaning to establish 天 (天, tian=t'ien, heaven). This character is a combination of "a big man" 大 (大, da, big) and the one and only and higher 一 (一, yi, one). In other words, it expresses something higher than the highest person. The common person or man is expressed as bending his waist like this: 亻 (人, ren, human).

When expressed as 大 (大, da, big), it means someone more powerful than a common man. Therefore, 天 (天, tian=t'ien, heaven) means someone higher than the big man, the one and only being, that is the God who lives in Heaven. Therefore, this letter is currently being used as a meaning for Heaven, Day, or God.

The oldest altar for worshiping the God of Heaven (5500–5000 years ago) <Liaoning Provincial Museum>

Temple of Heaven. First constructed in 1420, Beijing: The place where the emperors would celebrate the God of Heaven and pray for good harvest.

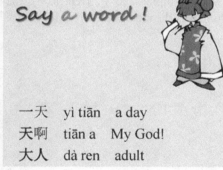

Say a word!

一天	yì tiān	a day
天啊	tiān a	My God!
大人	dà ren	adult

The most important principles in the universe: Heaven, Human, and Earth

There were three subjects that ancient East Asians considered to be the most important things in the universe. The principles are: Heaven, the Earth, and People.

Heaven (天, tian=t'ien, heaven) means the most supreme God, the Earth (地, di, earth) means mother earth where all living things are grown, and the People (人, ren, human) means the most important living being between heaven and mother earth.

The monument features the three supreme existences of the Universe: Heaven (天), Earth(地), and Human (人)— and the five basic elements of the universe: water(水), fire(火), iron (金), wood(木), soil(土) (14th-19th century)

<National Folk Museum of Korea >

仨 (仁, ren, love) reflects such a philosophy. This character has two lines: 二, and has a human (兀 人, ren, human). These symbols mean all three elements, Heaven, Earth, and People.

仁 (ren, love) does not only imply three elements, but also means "sincere love" for them. Confucius (552–479 BC) emphasized 仁 (ren, love), the sincere love of Heaven, Earth and Human as the most ideal virtue for a wise man to have.

Brick sculptures described of the divine people and animals in heaven. They abide by the order of the universe (AD 420-589) <National Museum of China>

2. THE KING WHO IS THE AGENT OF HEAVEN

The King connects Heaven and Earth. The trinity of Heaven, Earth and Human is also reflected in the character which means king: 王 (王, wang, king).

The three horizontal lines mean sky, human and earth, and the vertical line means the connection of the three elements each other. So this word is interpreted as the person who connects heaven and earth, the holy king.

On the other hand, I think this character depicts a big man (大) wearing something like a flat hat (━), who is standing on a flat platform (━) and with his arms and legs spread widely, ordering others.

Ancient East Asian civilizations were discovered in the North Eastern area of China. Sculptures of ancient kings (or Shamans) unearthed at these archaeological sites show that they wore headdresses which were flat. The meaning of the flat shape could be to show that this person is " a big man who can connect Heaven and Earth and Human."

In ancient China, the king thought to himself as the center of the world.

央 (央, yang, middle) consists of the king 大 (da, big), and the H-shaped symbol that means from border to border. Putting these symbols together, we can see the symbol means the king who reigns over the whole land.

This king had a variety of decorations on his head to show he was something special.

The figures of Kings or Priests in ancient China (Neolithic era). Their heads are flat. <Liaoning Provincial Museum>

The ancient Korean king's golden crown decoration of flowers and vines. (6th century) <National Museum of Korea >

漢 (英, ying, flower) means king of the world, standing with beautiful decorations of plants and flowers on his head. Nowadays this character means 'England,' because the pronunciation of the two words is very similar (Yīngguó).

A hat adorned with flowers worn by a Korean shaman. In ancient times, the shaman was as high as a king. <Cultural Heritage Administration of Korea >

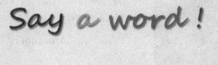

大王	dà wáng	Great king
中央	zhōng yāng	Centre
英国	Yīng guó	England
		(United Kingdom)

The King who wears a shining crown

Performing regular religious ceremonies for the gods was one of the major duties of the kings of East Asian countries.

光 (光, guang, light) This character has two components, a crown shining bright ⬇ and a person kneeling in front of it ⬇. This character depicts a king wearing a crown kneeling at an important ceremony asking god for guidance.

An ancient king (3,000 years ago) wearing a crown and kneeling, depicting the character light "光" <Yinxu Museum>

Bright gold crown used by the ancient Korean king (5th-6th century)

<National Museum of Korea >

The King wearing yellow jade decorations

The king wearing the crown also treasured jade, which was considered even more valuable than gold in East Asia.

黄 (黄, 黄, huang, yellow) depicts a man of high position 大 (大, da, big) standing proudly and wearing a decoration around his waist. In those times, the man in high positions wore a waist decoration carved in jade.

Dragon carving ornament (13th -11th century BC) <Shanghai Museum>

How did this character come to mean "yellow"? Many jade decorations were discovered at the tombs of ancient aristocrats or kings in Northeast China. Among the jade decoarions, there are ones that a person wore around his waist just like this: 黄. The part of the decoration which covers the wearer's belly is yellow.

Cloud-shaped waist ornament (13th -11th century BC) <Shanghai Museum>

Yellow jade which is rectangular or circle in shape shines like the sun in daylight. Since it reflects the sun which is one of the most worshiped gods, people have considered it very sacred.

Chinese Emperor (Qing Dynasty, 1678-1735) traditionally dressed in yellow clothes.

Bronze vessel with an inlaid hunting scene (6th century-476 BC) The ancient Chinese regarded the Earth as the mother of all living things. <Shanghai Museum>

Ceremony to pray to the earth

Along with Heaven, the Earth was an object of worship. The people who developed the Hanzi system built an earthen pillar 土 土 (土, tu, earth). In fact, the pillar means ten (十, shi, ten) which also means 'many'. So we can see this character describes the land from which many creatures sprout.

The "Shuo Wen Jie Zi (Explanation of Chinese Characters)" written about 2,000 years ago says that " 'Tu' means that earth regurgitates living things." In other words, all the living things came from the Earth. Therefore, in ancient society, it was very important to worship Mother Earth which gave birth to all living things.

If the spirit tablet or altar 示 (示, shi=shih, show) is added next to the earth, the meaning becomes 'society' 社 (社, she, god of the earth, society).

When the ancient Chinese performed the ceremonies, they built an altar out of earth and lit a fire on top of the high altar. Many people gathered around and spent a serious yet joyful time. Therefore, the connotation of the character evolved to be a society or a group or where people gather.

The square altar of earth-god. In the past, people thought of heaven as a circle and the earth as a square. (14ᵗʰ-19ᵗʰ century, Seoul) < Cultural Heritage Administration of Korea >

Soil & Jade, the soul of the earth

Ancient eastern people worshiped the earth. So, they tried to preserve the natural land rather than cultivate and develop it. They thought of the earth as their mother because all the creatures come from the earth.

里 (里, li, place, inside)

The upper one ⊕ (田, tian=t'ien, field) means field divided into four places, and lower one ± (土, tu, soil) means the earth on which some corps are rising, and it also means an altar people gathering. The whole character means the village where people gather in the field, performing rites.

In the past, people considered that the earth of their hometown would protect them, and they worshiped the god of their own territory by building an altar. This god of hometown would judge the people of the village whether to go to Heaven or to go to hell.

理 (理, li, manage, reason) The left side of the symbol 王 (玉, yu=yü, jade) is a jade bead, and the right side 里 is a village where people live together.

The ancient people believed that the jade are so pure than any other existences of the earth, and they believed that the jade is a soul of the land which can defeat the evil spirits. Because jade (玉) can judge people of the village with the spirit of the earth (土), 理 is used as a meaning of control, manage, reason etc.

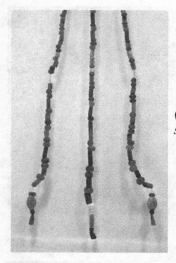

A necklace made of jade and glass beads (206 BC - AD 8) <Liaoning Provincial Museum>

Necklace of jade and glass beads (14th-19th century) <National Museum of Korea >

Say a word!

土地   tǔ dì   land

社会   shè huì   society

灯光   dēng guāng   lamplight

这里   zhè lǐ   here

Beautiful jewelry made of jade and gold. Jade was a treasure that East Asians worshiped as the spirit of the earth. (5th-6th century) < Gongju National Museum of Korea >

3. ARISTOCRATS WEAR HORNS

The Shaman shakes bells and conducts the ceremony

告 告 (告, gao, inform) is interpreted by the scholars as "bell used by the king." The bottom part 廿 (口, kou, mouth) shows a widely opened mouth, the body of the bell and 屮 this part shows the pendulum of the bell.

A bronze bell which was used for religious ceremonies during Shang Dynasty (16th-11th century BC) <Yinxu Museum>

Many bronze bells were discovered in the tombs of the kings and shamans from the Bronze Age in China. During Shang Dynasty (1600-1046 BC), people who could ring the bells were upper class people such as kings or shamans. They would shake the bells and tell the prophecy from gods. Therefore now this character means "to inform".

Meaning of gods in bronze plates

The ancient shamans (or kings) also offered animal sacrifices such as cows or lambs to the gods. These sacrifices were prepared in the huge bronze plates. 監 監 (監, 监, jian=chien, supervise) This character shows the ceremonial plate, 屮 and a figure who is kneeling in front of the plate and watching it very attentively 見 (見, 见, jian=chien, see; meet with). Inside the ceremonial plate, there is a stroke (✍), which means the sacrifice. This character shows how careful and attentive he is.

Bronze containers for rituals (11ᵗʰ-10ᵗʰ century BC) <Beijing Capital Museum>

Smelling the food and celebrating their ancestors

The Kings of ancient China prohibited the common people from celebrating the Heavenly God, because they regarded the right to worship the Heavenly God as a privilege of the king. Instead, the Kings allowed the people to worship their own ancestors.

Man sitting on his knees (221-206 BC) <National Museum of China>

鄉(鄉, 乡, xiang=hsiang, countryside) describes the vessel with high leg 豆 (豆, dou, beans) which is filled with an offering and two people who are watching over the vessel.

They are smelling the precious offering and celebrating a ceremony.

In the past this character meant "a ceremony for the ancestors". Now, this character means "home" or "country home". The location where people celebrate ceremony for "ancestors" is the place they came from — their physical and spiritual "home country".

At that time, people used an elevated plate 豆 for ceremonies. In Korea, widely influenced by China in the past, people still use elevated plates for the ceremonies.

Bronze bowls with a high pedestal (8th-7th century BC) <Liaoning Provincial Museum>

Say a word !

告诉	gào su	tell
再见	zài jiàn	say goodbye
家乡	jiā xiāng	hometown

A beautiful Shaman wearing lamb's horns

Shamans with headdress performing the ceremony (403- 221 BC) <Beijing Capital Museum>

During the times when Chinese characters were being invented, the shamans or kings wore headdresses decorated with animal horns or feathers. When they were dressed in elaborate headdresses and luxurious clothes, they personified the word "beauty" themselves.

This is the origin of the character 美 (美, mei, beautiful).

A big person 大 (大, da, big) is wearing a sheep's horn 羊 (羊, yang, sheep) in this character. It describes a King standing proudly wearing a headdress of sheep's horn. On the other hand, because the sheep means God's righteousness, the character can also mean 'the man of God – the King'.

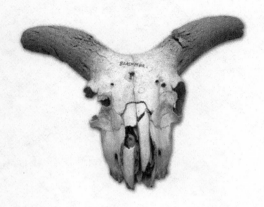

A sheep's head dedicated to sacrifice (1300-1046 BC) <Yinxu Museum>

4. The Religious Ceremony With Rice, Wine, Meat And Blood

The vassals standing in their proper places

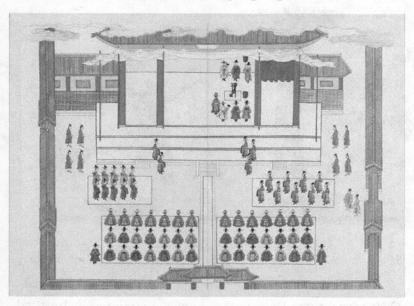

The coronation ceremony of Prince. The officials at the royal court were seated according to their status. The ceremonial practices were conducted in accordance with 13 procedures. Early 19ᵗʰ century in Korea. < National Palace Museum of Korea >

Vassals in East Asia had to wear clothes in different colors depending on their status. Even when the memorial service was held at the royal palace, they had to be placed in a designated location. 㑉 (位, wei, position; location) There is a man on the left side bending his waist 刀 (人, ren, human, people), and a well-dressed nobleman standing on the right side 㑉(立, li, stand). When the ceremonies were held in the royal court, the officials stood in position according to their status.

Wine and meat brings fortune

Even in present times, in East Asia, when one offers a religious ceremony to his ancestors, he offers an alcohol.

㣺 福 (福, fu, blessing, good fortune)
This character shows on the left a spirit tablet 示, on the right an alcohol glass with a tall neck 酉, and beneath, a hand holding the cup 又. This shows a person holding an alcohol cup with both hands in front of a spirit tablet.

Wine vessels used in sacrifices (16ᵗʰ-11ᵗʰ century BC) <Yinxu Museum>

Offering wine to the ancestors or gods signifies good crops and gratitude towards the ancestors and gods for giving abundance. Also, it enables people to be intoxicated, which could gie the impression of communicating with their gods.

Did they drink just regular wine? No, their wines were those which contained the spirit of their ancestors after the ceremony, and therefore, "good fortune (福, fu) ".

The King is drinking the wine of 'Good fortune' in the ceremony. <Lee Royal Family Association, Korea >

鐏 (尊, zun, respect)

At the top of the character, there is a cup of wine酋, and below is the hand holding the cup with the fingers bent 寸 (寸, cun=ts'un, unit of length, approximately 3cm). It shows that one gives wine to the honorable spirits of the ancestors or gods. Nowadays, this character means 'respect'.

*A noble offers up a glass of wine to the gods in the royal rites process. <
Lee Royal Family Association, Korea >*

Say a word !

美国	Měi guó	America (the USA)
位置	wèi zhi	location; position
幸福	xìng fú	happiness
尊敬	zūn jìng	respect

Government official offers celebratory prayer

After offering wine to the ancestral spirits, the government official read out celebratory prayers. 㕚 祝 (祝, zhu, express good wishes): this symbol shows a man kneeling (𠂤) in front of a spirit tablet (示) and opening his mouth (ㅂ). He is saying prayers in front of the god.

The present Chinese call themselves "Han nationality". The Han (漢, 汉) Dynasty dates back to 206 BC - AD 220.

The first emperor of the Han Dynasty, Liu Bang, united China. There is a record which says that he worshiped the god of war and ordered "the government official who prays for blessing" to pray to this god. Thus it was customary for a government official to read prayers out loud.

Wine Vessel (11th Century BC)
<Shanghai Museum>

Bow down to god

East Asian people would kneel down in front of others to indicate their modesty and humility. Today, the Japanese and Korean still preserve such a custom. They usually sit on their knees in the presence of their elders.

㣇川 (比, bi, compare) shows two people raising their hands and bowing down on their knees simultaneously. By following others while showing a polite appearance, people compare themselves to each other.

川 (北, bei, north) means two people standing opposite to each other. One does not follow the other's politeness.

When people see the sun in the south, the opposite side is the north. So this means 'north'. And when the flesh 肰 (肉, rou, flesh) is added to this character 肰 (背, bei, back; go against), it means 'back', 'betrayal'.

A plate containing blood

The kings of ancient East Asia would hold a ceremony when they met for treaties. They would fill the ceremonial cauldron with the blood of the sacrificed animal. Afterwards, they would drink the blood or smear the blood over their lips. 㞢 盃 (血, xie=hsieh, blood)

In this character, we can see a ceremonial cauldron 㞢 and a spot ᛁ. This spot symbolizes the ceremonial meat or ceremonial blood.

Lieges are bowing down on their knees at the same time in the royal court. < Lee Royal Family Association, Korea >

The ancient Chinese history book "Shi Ji" says: "When people gathered to make a promise, they would drink a little of the sacrifice's blood to show their sincerity."

Bronze wine vessel with oxen design (1046–771 BC) <National Museum of China>

Vessel of a high stand, symbolizing respect to the gods. Commonly used in ancient Korea (about 5ᵗʰ century) <National Folk Museum of Korea >

益(益, yi, benefit, increase) This is a water vessel with abundant water flowing, describing the water filled and overflowed in the vessel of high stand. This picture represents the meaning of 'increase', 'benefit'.

Say a word !

祝贺	zhù hè	congratulate
比较	bǐ jiào	compare
北京	Běi jīng	Beijing
牛肉	niú ròu	beef
利益	lì yì	benefit

5. ANIMAL SACRIFICES FOR RELIGIOUS CEREMONIES

Various animals were used for ceremonial sacrifice

The ancient Chinese kings used large animals for ceremonial sacrifices. The cow was one of the important animal sacrifices. 牣 牣 (物, wu, thing) To the left of the character, there is a character which symbolizes the head of the cow 牜 (牛, niu, cattle), to the right, there is a character 刁 which symbolizes the knife 刁 (刀, dao, knife), and there are blood splattered (ᶦ). This character depicts cutting a cow with a knife.

Bronze Knife (13ᵗʰ-11ᵗʰ century BC) <Yinxu Museum>

During the Shang (商) Dynasty (1600–1046 BC), the aristocrats sacrificed many animals for ceremonies. According to the records, the emperor's court also had many luxurious and grand ceremonies. At one occasion, hundreds of cows were sacrificed. Various sacrifices were offered other than cows at these ceremonies as well. So, 物 (物, wu) changed its meaning from "sacrifice" to "things."

Bronze Wine Vessel (1300- 1046 BC) <National Museum of China>

Meat for rituals prepared carefully

The meat for rituals would be cut in equal shapes and prepared carefully. The next character 多 (多, duo, many) means sacrificial meat stacked high. This is the origin of "many".

Offerings sacrificed for royal ancestral rites. There are multiple layers of meat on the altar.

The meat sacrificed for the rites is considered very sacred. After the ceremony, the sacrificial meat is delivered to the nobles in whom the King trusts.

有 (有, you, have) On top of the symbol is the right hand 又 (又, you, again) delivering sacrificial offerings to the others repeatedly, and the below 肉 (肉, rou, flesh) is the sacrificed meat. Because the meat belongs to the King or owners, 有 (有, you, have) this character was used as 'to have'.

The carcases of large animals like cows or sheep were cut up to fit inside the cauldron. After the ritual, the cauldron would be emptied using a round ladle. 員員

(員, 员, yuan=yüan, member) shows using a round ladle **o** to scoop up something from the bronze cauldron.員 After the ceremony the King shared the contents cooked in the bronze cauldron with his court. Therefore, the character 員 (员, yuan, member) came to mean people belonging to the organization, or civil servants.

Bronze container and scoop for ritual (1300- 1046 BC) <Yinxu Museum>

Say a word !

动**物**	dòng wù	animal
牛**奶**	niú nǎi	milk
多少	duō shao	how much
没有	méi yǒu	not have
服务**员**	fú wù yuán	waiter

Tigers and dogs as ritual sacrifices

The sacrifices for ceremonies were not only meat 𣎆 (肉, rou, flesh). Among the elements of the symbol "鼡" (獻, 献, xian=hsien, offer, dedicate), 𧆨 is the head of a tiger roaring 𧆨 (虎, hu, tiger). Why is the head of a tiger on top of the ceremonial cauldron? And what about the animal next to it 犭 which is similar to the dog?

In ancient China, the head of a prisoner of war or a precious animal might also be offered to the king or the gods. One of the discoveries from ancient sites shows a human head still inside a bronze cauldron. The character shows a head of precious animals such as a tiger, and maybe even a dog was used as sacrifice.

Tiger-shaped handle of Bronze vessel (5 century-3 century BC) <Beijing Capital Museum>

Bronze vessel containing a human skull (1300-1046 BC) <Yinxu Museum>

A Ceremony of a Cow in Water

Some ceremonies were performed in the palace, using the precious bronze plates; some others were performed outside in nature.

𣎆 (沉, chen, sink) is a combination of a cow's head ♥ (牛, niu, cattle) and a flowing river 𠇗. In the book of "Zhou Li" which records the manners and etiquettes of ancient times, a record shows that "they drowned a lynx and made an offering of it during the ceremony for the mountain, river and the lake." The purpose of drowning animals or dipping them in the water is to show people's sincerity toward the god.

Big Axe used for cutting sacrificial animals (18ᵗʰ century-16ᵗʰ century BC) <Shanghai Museum>

6. Messengers of God: Bronze, and Bones

Message of god sent through bronze plate

The king and the aristocrats used a huge bronze cauldron for ceremonies. To have a cracked or deformed cauldron was considered to be very bad luck. Since the bronze cauldron was sacred, if it were ruined, they would have shouted "Bu (no) !" and this became the origin of the meaning of the word today as "no" or "forbidden"丕 (不, bu, no; not). The original shape of this character was the ceremonial cup (杯, bei, cup) with three legs which were distorted. The three legs represent 'Heaven, Human, Earth', and the distortion of these three legs means 'bad luck', 'evil'.

It was not easy to make a model of bronzeware with mud or wax. When the model for molding was deformed, people thought it was the sign of evil.

Bronze wine cup with three legs used for Korean royal ceremony. (14th-19th century) <National Museum of Korea >

If the vessels were not perfect, it was believed that God would refuse to accept the ceremony. 否 (否, fou, deny) In comparison with the above one 丕 (不, bu, no; not), this character is added of 口

(口, kou, mouse) which means 'mouse' or 'speaking'. God is speaking not to accept the imperfect ceremony.

A huge bronze cauldron with three legs (1046-771 BC) <National Museum of China>

Sacred Bones which show the god's anger and joy

The Shang Dynasty people who made ancient Chinese characters believed that they could tell a fortune by grilling a turtle's shell or a cow's flat shoulder bone over the fire. When the bones were heated over the fire, at one point cracks would appear on the surface and make crackling sounds.

(禍, 祸, huo, misfortune) shows an altar and a flat bone, which has a crack (ㅓ) and mouse () on it.

The people then judged good or bad luck according to the direction of the crack. The Shang Dynasty people worshiped the right side, however,

⺊ shows the crack towards the left. Therefore they used this character as "misfortune/disaster". This character's shape was gradually developed to 禍 (禍, 祸, huo, misfortune) adding the altar (示, shi, show) left, emphasizing the God's will.

Turtle's shell and a cow's flat blade used for divination (16ᵗʰ-11ᵗʰ century BC) <Yinxu Museum>

Say a word !

贡献	gòng xiàn	devote
老虎	lǎo hǔ	tiger
沉默	chén mò	be silent
干杯	gān bēi	drink a toast
车祸	chē huò	traffic accident
表示	biǎo shì	express

7. THE PEOPLE FROM THE SUN AND THE STARS

The Sun; the god over all living things

People who made Chinese characters worshiped light, brightness, and the sun. They regarded the sun as the origin for all life forms and therefore they worshiped the sun. Also, they revered all shining entities in the sky such as the moon and the stars. They observed the celestial bodies and tried to find meanings. Such philosophy is reflected in the Chinese characters.

Bronze mirror symbolizing sun. The priest who was the representative of Heaven wore this mirror at the sacrificial rites (16th-11th century BC) <Yinxu Museum>

According to the explanation of "Shuo Wen Jie Zi" in Ancient Chinese, the character of "Spring" 齃 (春, chun, spring) means "to push." Where did this meaning come from? This character describes the grasses on the top ΨΨ (草, cao-ts'ao, grass), and a sprout in the middle, which is coming out on the ground ⍾, and the sun ⊖ (日, ri, sun; day). The sun is pushing the sprout to pierce the ground, helping it to grow.

49

After the cold goes away, spring comes, bringing warm sunlight and helping the new sprouts to come up to the surface of the earth. The ancient people saw this and thought, "the sun helps to push the new sprouts up to the surface."

The stars as gods in heaven

For ancient East Asian people, nature was to be revered. When they gazed upon the clear night skies and many stars above, they thought that the stars were like spirits of people.

曐 星 (星, xing=hsing star) When we see this character, it shows the green plants (屮) coming up from the earth (土), which symbolizes full of life 坣 (生, sheng, to live, life), and stars scattered around it 晶 (晶, jing, brilliant; crystal). In ancient dictionary, it was explained that "stars are spirits of all living things". According to the explanations, the stars or the constellations are related to the spirits of living things. Why did the ancient people connect the stars with the spirit?

A bronze mirror used by a shaman of Korea. There are the Sun and the Moon above, and the Big Dipper below. In ancient times, a shaman was a high priest in charge of rites. <National Folk Museum of Korea >

People worshiped the stars as spirits of all creation, and in Taoism, the North Star was considered the place where the Heaven God (天, Tian=t'ien) stayed.

In the eastern part of ancient China, Shandong, during 770 BC – 403 BC, there was a powerful kingdom of Qi (=Ch'i). There lived King Jing-Gong, who mourned when he saw a comet during the 33rd year of his reign or 515 BC. His royal subjects also cried with him. This is because the King mourned a death of a great man when he saw the comet fall.

Therefore, the reason there is the character 甤 (生, sheng, to live, life), which means life/birth甦 (星, xing=hsing star), is because people thought that Heaven (天, tian=t'ien, Heaven, God) was the origin of all living things.

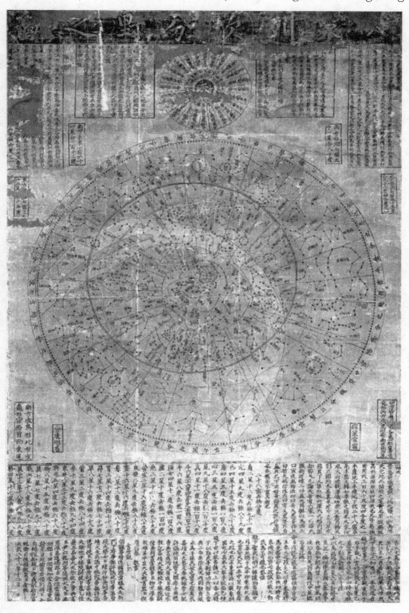

The constellation originally made of lithography in 14th century, reprinted in the year 1571. < National Palace Museum of Korea >

方 (七, qi=ch'i, seven) is a Big Dipper. The ancient people believed that the seven stars of the Big Dipper are gods, and that they were responsible for farming and human life.

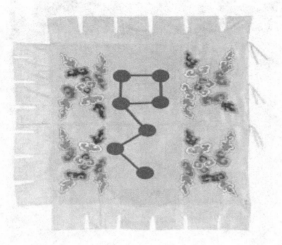

The flag of Big Dipper. It was a prestigious flag which was held in front of the king's wagon. (14th-19th century)

< National Palace Museum of Korea >

Say a word!

青春	qīng chūn	youth
日本	Rì běn	Japan
星期	xīng qī	week
学生	xué sheng	student
七月	qī yuè	July

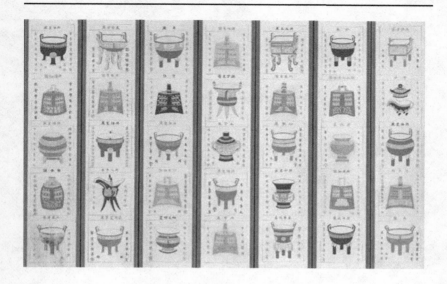

Various utensils used in rites (19ᵗʰ century) < National Palace Museum of Korea >

PART 2. 人 (REN) HUMAN

1. PEOPLE

A person with his back bent

It is very typical and area-specific of Asia to bow down to a person who is of higher rank to you. In Japan and Korea, people still bow to show respect and courtesy.

ㅅ 几 (人, ren, human) implies a profile of a person with his back bent, expressing the humility.

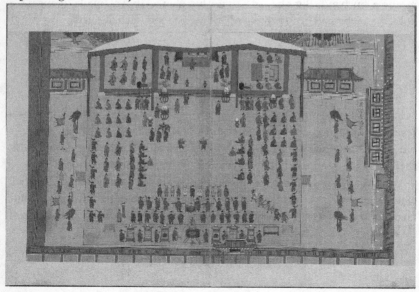

At the banquet in 1719, lieges bowing down and folding their hands in front of the king. <National Museum of Korea >

A person who is of higher rank and proud is expressed in a front view 大 (大, da, big) without bowing to others.

夫 (夫, fu, husband) is a man wearing his hair in a knot. Because the married man tied up his hair with a rod-like hairpin, this character now means a husband. But the first time this character was made, it meant a nobleman who had been promoted and who stood with dignity.

A wise old man with long hair and a kid with a "soft" head

長 (長, 长, zhang, chang, older; long) An old man with his long hair is handling something skillfully. The old man is good at many things as a result of all his experience. The eastern people considered respect for the older person as one of the most important virtues, so they even didn't cut their hair because the hair is the remnant of the old parents.

老 (老, lao, old) describes an old person bending his back wearing an elaborate head-dress 耂, and a child or a man bowing to him ヒ. Although this character is used as the old person now, the original meaning was a person of no ordinary status; an older bureaucrat.

A nobleman wearing a topknot with a rod-like hairpin. Etching by Elizabeth Keith (1887~1956). <National Folk Museum of Korea >

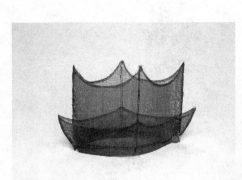

Elaborate head-dress and an old man who is wearing it; the traditional hat old men usually wore. (14ᵗʰ-19ᵗʰ century) <The Academy of Korean Studies>

A child is depicted as 兒 (兒, 儿, er=erh, child). 儿 (人, ren, human) means people, then what does ⊖ mean? Some say it means a child crying to the sky and some say that the bones of the head are not formed yet (as in a boy's head).

A person who goes ahead; the ancestor

How did the Chinese refer to people who have passed away, the ancestors, in other words? They drew it like this: 先 (先, xian=hsien, earlier, elder generation).

The top part 止 (止, zhi=chih, stop) is the footprint going forth over a base line —, and the bottom part 儿 (人, ren, human) means a person. That is, someone following the footsteps of the person who went before him/her.

Sage: One who listens

聖 (聖, 圣, sheng, holy, sage) reflects the ancient Chinese thoughts about the holy person (sage). This symbol is composed of a person whose position is low 人 (人, ren, human) and on the top an ear 耳 (耳, er, ear), and a mouth 口 (口, kou, mouse) next to them. It shows someone listening to what others are saying.

In his book "Chun Qiu", Confucius emphasizes how important it is to listen well to others, especially the heavenly God. This is why Confucius who listened attentively is regarded as "Holy Man" or "Sage".

Confucius said that "At age sixty, I heard and followed (the words from the Heavens)." In other words, he is confessing that it took him sixty years to hear Heaven's command.

Say a word!

丈夫	zhàng fu	husband
校长	xiào zhǎng	principal
老师	lǎo shī	teacher
儿子	ér zi	son
先生	xiān sheng	Mr
禁止	jìn zhǐ	forbid

Representative saints of China, Confucius (above, 551-479 BC) and Laozi (below, 604-531 BC). According to legend, their ears were very big. <National Museum of China>

Woman with her knees bent

About 3,000 years ago, the Shang Dynasty people sat on their knees in front of elder people, and they regarded this sitting position polite. Women especially, often sat in this way.

(女, nü, woman) represents a woman sitting on her knees.

Statue of Lady (206 BC – AD 8) <Shanghai Museum>

A Visitor to the house

(安, an, peaceful) is composed of a house (入, ru, enter), and a woman sitting on her knees (女, nü, woman). The woman is sitting comfortably at home. It seems that the house and wife were the symbols of stability for men.

Someone came to such a peaceful house. (客, ke=k'e, visitor) describes a person's foot upside down in front of the door . The character shows the lady of the house inside her home, and a visitor to the house.

A party scene. Women musicians kneeling and playing instruments (403-221 BC) <Shanghai Museum>

圣经	shèng jīng	the Bible
耳朵	ěr duo	ear
女儿	nǚ ér	daughter
安全	ān quán	safe
入口	rù kǒu	entrance
客人	kè rén	visitor

2. Family Dynamics

Ancestors and sacrifices

祖 (祖, zu, ancestor) shows a ceremonial plate 且 (且, qie=ch'ieh, and). In early Chinese, the character 且 (qie=ch'ieh, and) was used to mean ancestor. However, the original meaning of the character was a ceremonial plate which was used to contain meats for ceremony to pay respects to the ancestors.

Since the meat was sacred, a sacrifice to be eaten by the spirit of ancestors, many years afterwards the spirit tablet 示 (shi, show) was added to the character, and came to mean ancestor 祖 (祖, zu, ancestor).

A ceremonial plate for kings to use when honoring the ancestors. One is used to steam organs from cows, pigs, or lambs in there and offer them to the gods or ancestors 祖 (zu, ancestor). <The Royal Ancestral Shrine of Korea>

Scene of consecrating sacrifice on the plate to the ancestral spirits.
<The Royal Ancestral Shrine of Korea>

The titular King of Korea is consecrating wine to the ancestral spirits.
<The Royal Ancestral Shrine of Korea>

Long ago, the sacrificial rites of China were introduced into Korea and they continue to be practiced to this day. <The Royal Ancestral Shrine of Korea>

Father with jade panel: Authority

The symbol for "Father" 㸚 (父, fu, father) shows a person holding something long 丨 in his hand 㐅 (又, you, again). According to "Shuo Wen Jie Zi," this shows the authority figure's hand holding a whip for teaching and punishment.

However, the authority figure is not just holding a plain whip. He is holding a Jade Panel, which symbolizes power and authority of kings and aristocrats. So the thing he is holding is not merely a whip but a symbol of power.

Jade scepter symbolizing the authority of the priests or nobles (21th century-16th century BC) <Shanghai Museum>

Ancient Japanese nobility holding jade scepters <Osaka Museum of History, Japan>

Wife, mother

As mentioned before, 凡 (女, nü, woman; daughter) depicts a young woman sitting on her knees and holding her hands together politely. When she grows up, she becomes a man's wife. The difference between the unmarried young woman and the married woman is the hairstyle.

農 (妻, qi=ch'i, wife) depicts a woman 凡 who is sitting on her knees with her hair ψ held by a hand ⇒. In the past, when a woman got married, she raised her hair up in a pigtail and fixed it with a rod-like hairpin. Thus this character means a 'married woman' or a 'wife'.

Hairpins made of bone (13th century-11th century BC) <Yinxu Museum>

祖先	zǔ xiān	ancestors
而且	ér qiě	and what's more
父亲	fù qīn	father
妻子	qī zi	wife

When a woman gave birth to a child, she nursed the baby; 𢍑 (母, mu, mother) shows a woman with "breasts" so she can take care of her baby.

The married woman let down her hair when she was sleeping and put it again in every morning.

𢑻 (每, mei, every; each) means a mother whose rich hair is pulled up. Because mothers have to manage their hair every day, this character became to represent 'every', 'each'.

A very delicately decorated hairdo seems like a wave; 𣲐 (海, hai, sea) consists of a water flow 𣱱 (水, shui, water) and a mother with her hair up 𣫫 (母, mu, mother). In the past, women avoided ever cutting their hair, so their long hair flowed like a flourishing wave, and the symbol came to mean the 'sea'.

Women on swings. Married women wore their hair in a bun and unmarried women wore their hair long. (18th century, Korea) < National Palace Museum of Korea >

A woman with her hair decorated (18th century, Korea) <National Museum of Korea >

Various ornaments made of bone (13th century-11th century BC) <Yinxu Museum>

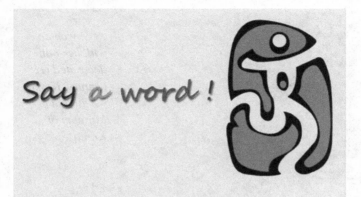

母亲	mǔ qīn	mother
每年	měi nián	every year
大海	dà hǎi	sea and ocean
水果	shuǐ guǒ	fruit

Elder brother gives orders; younger brother obeys

The first born son had a privilege as the inheritor of the parents' family fortune. In return, the oldest son was responsible for the ceremonies of ancestors and parents. With such privilege, the eldest son had power over his younger siblings. Therefore, the eldest son often ordered his younger siblings around. 兄 (兄, xiong=hsiung, elder brother) describes elder brother, which combines a ㅂ (口, kou, mouse) and a person 儿 (人, ren, human). Together, they symbolize "a person who speaks or gives orders". If the spirit tablet or altar 示 (示, shi=shih, show) is added to the left 祝, (祝, zhu, wish), it means the eldest brother who represents the group praying or calling a blessing from God.

Then, how can the younger brother be depicted? The creator(s) of Hanzi thought about the sequence of brothers. The character 弟 (弟, di, younger brother) shows a spear in the middle (戈), and a rope winding the spear (乙). The reason for winding the spear is to prevent slippage and to make sure the spear will not break. This character came to mean "younger brother" because of the meaning of winding order, or sequence.

When you wind a rope around the spear, you have to do it in an orderly way. Therefore, it symbolizes the order in the ages of the siblings.

The represent of a village is reading a written prayer to God in the early 20th century <National Folk Museum of Korea >

The character 第 (di, auxiliary word for ordinal numbers) is also from this character under the same logic. The top of this character means bamboo (竹), the material of spear, and below is the rope which winds the spear. For example, 第一 (di yi) means 'the first' (the first rope of the spear), 第二 (di er) means 'the second'.

Man sitting on his knees (13th century-11th century BC) <National Museum of China>

73

Grandchild

In ancient times people made a rope by combining straws one after another. When they made ropes, they thought of the ropes as symbolizing the descendants because of how the rope continues on. The 孫 (孫, 孙, sun, grandchild) reflects their thoughts. The character symbolizes "grandchild" by combining child 子 (子, zi=tzu, child) and rope 絲 (絲, 丝, si=ssu, silk). These two combinations came to mean future generation, the descendants, or a grandchild.

兄弟	xiōng dì	brother
第一	dì yī	first
孙子	sūn zi	grandson
丝毫	sī háo	slightest

Pregnancy and breastfeeding

What do you think 身 (身, shen, body) is? It used to mean a pregnant woman with a child inside her. Now it means "body".

At long last, the woman gives birth to a baby.

育 describes a woman giving birth to a child 子 (子, zi=tzu, child), bleeding blood . This character has changed to 育 (育, yu=yü, give birth to, bring up), a newborn child and flesh (肉, rou, flesh), meaning that a new born child is gradually growing up.

After giving birth, she breastfeeds the baby.

好 shows a mother with her breast out to feed the baby 母 and the baby 子 trying to suckle. A mother embracing the child feels so happy, this character means 'good', 'like'.

And the shape was also changed as 🙏 (好, hao, good;love).

Women collecting mulberry leaves (403-221 BC) <Shanghai Museum>

Raising the baby or abandoning the baby

In ancient East Asia, women often carried their children on their backs. The baby feels protected and attached to the mother in this way 保 (保, bao, protect). This symbol combines a human 𠆢 (人, ren, human) with a child on the right 子 (子, zi=tzu, child) and two points ⼃ which indicate a pair of hands holding the child. It shows a human carrying a child on his/her back. Now the word has come to mean to "protect".

On the other hand, 棄 (棄, 弃, qi=ch'i, abandon) shows a different scene. A child 子 (子, zi=tzu, child), just born with blood on the skin ⼃, is on top of a straw basket 𠀠 (其, qi=ch'i, that) and two hands ⼋ are holding them from below. What is going on?

Many people had to abandon their babies due to illness or famine when food was scarce. This character describes such a sad situation. Someone is throwing his/her baby in the basket.

A mother carrying a baby on her back. Traditionally, Koreans raised babies on their back. 18ᵗʰ century <National Museum of Korea >

Traditional straw basket <Samcheok Municipal Museum of Korea>

Say a word!

身体　shēn tǐ　body

教育　jiào yù　education

好吃　hǎo chī　Good taste

保证　bǎo zhèng　guarantee

放弃　fàng qì　give … up

其实　qí shí　actually

3. BODY PARTS

Face/Head and eyes

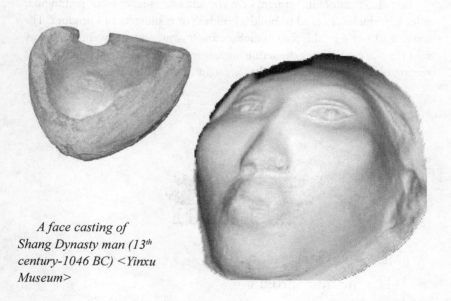 (面, mian=mien, face) can be divided into a person's face 𝒪 and his/her eyes 𝒪 (目, mu, eye).

A face casting of Shang Dynasty man (13ᵗʰ century-1046 BC) <Yinxu Museum>

🖋 目 (目, mu, eye) is an eye which is slit. The sculptures of the Shang Dynasty (16th–11th BC) show people with such slit-shaped eyes.

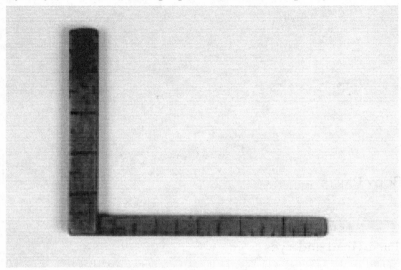

Old rectangular ruler <National Folk Museum of Korea >

直 (直, 直, zhi=chih, straight) On the left side is an ancient rectangular ruler ∟, which was used to build a building or manufacture a product. The top is a 10 ✚ (十, shi, ten), which means 'many', and an eye in the below 目 (目, mu, eye). The craftsman is measuring something repeatedly with a rectangular ruler. It is now used as 'straight', 'honest'.

Say a word !

前面	qián mian	the front
节目	jié mù	program
一直	yì zhí	straight; always
十分	shí fēn	extremely

看 (看, kan, see; look at) The upside is the hand with 5 fingers 手 (手, shou, hand) shading the eye 目 (目, mu, eye). It looks like someone spreads a palm to block the sun and looks around.

見 (見, 见, jian=chien, see; meet with) consists of an eye 目 and a kneeling person 儿 (人, ren, human), depicting a subject sees up at the king or a senior, expressing his opinion.

A kneeling vassal (16ᵗʰ-11ᵗʰ century BC) <Yinxu Museum>

自 (自, zi=tzu, self) came to mean "self" in the present times but it used to mean a nose (鼻, bi, nose). This maybe because when one refers to himself/herself, he/she points toward the nose with the fingers.

Gilt silver mask (AD 916-1125) <Liaoning Provincial Museum>

⊞ (齒, 齿, chi=ch'ih, tooth) means teeth. We can see the teeth ᴗᴗ in the mouth ▢ (口, kou).

▢ looks like a smiling mouth. This character not only means a mouth, but also means the mouth of a bottle, the entrance of a house or a cave, and a hole, etc.

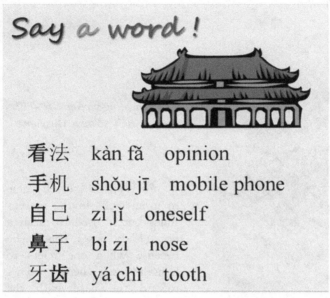

Say a word!

看法	kàn fǎ	opinion
手机	shǒu jī	mobile phone
自己	zì jǐ	oneself
鼻子	bí zi	nose
牙齿	yá chǐ	tooth

Right and Left hands

There are some mysterious commonalities in cultures from different parts of the world. In many cultures, including East and West, "right hand" came to mean positive while the "left hand" came to mean something negative. In China, when one says "you are thinking Left", it refers to wrong thinking.

Right hand 𰀁 (右, you, right) used to mean "help with god's hands".

Left hand 𰀂 (左, zuo, left) also used to mean "help of god". Both symbols used to mean "sacred help from god" but now the meaning has changed to "right" and "left".

The respect to the right is reflected in the difference of these two symbols. ㅂ (口, kou, mouse) in the character of the right means 'order', and ㅛ (工, gong, worker; industry). In the character meaning 'left,' it means just a 'tool (ruler)' or 'support'.

丿𠂛 (力, li, power) means the power of the right hand. And if a field is added on this character 𠂛 (男, nan, man), it means a man who cultivates farmland.

Three men working together with a shovel in a field. (19ᵗʰ century, Korea)

幼 (幼, you, young; under age) The left side means cocoons with silk 8 (丝, si=ssu, silk) and the right is an arm. Because the silk is very thin and easy to be cut, this character suggests the very weak power of a child's arm.

Putting the silkwork cocoons in boiling water, the ilk can be pulled out to make thread.
<Cultural Heritage Administration of Korea >

Weaving fabric on a loom < Cultural Heritage Administration of Korea>

Say a word!

右边　yòu bian　right
左边　zuǒ bian　left
工作　　gōng zuò　work
努力　nǔ lì　try hard
男女　nán nǔ　men and women
幼儿园　yòu' ér yuán
kindergarten

4. House, Food, and Clothes

House made out of hay

人 (人, ru, enter) is the shape of an ancient house. People back then dug a hollow in the ground and lived there or built a tree house to escape from the attacks of wild animals. 人 shows a house made of reeds or tall grass on the ground, and it evolves to signify "enter" or "income".

Ancient house made of reeds (the Stone Age) <Gongju Paleolith Museum, Korea>

月 (內, nei, inner) reflects the picture of a house with an open entrance. This means "inside".

House with doors

Not many people could afford wooden doors. Only high class government officials and upper class aristocratic people could afford doors on their houses.

門 (門, 门, men, door, gate) shows a two-leaf door in front of a big house.

Ancient House (About 5th century)
< Gyungju National Museum of Korea >

Traditional House with two-leaf door < Cultural Heritage Administration of Korea >

工 (工, gong, worker) It means a large tool that was widely used as a ruler or saw when constructing a building or making objects.

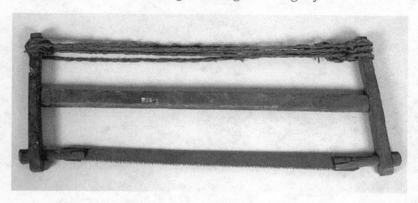

Traditional tool: There is a thread tied on the big frame and a saw underneath. <National Museum of Korea >

臣 (巨, ju=Chü, huge) It consists of a large handle and a ruler that was used to draw a straight line or a frame for fixing the saw. It is used as 'big' because it is long and wide.

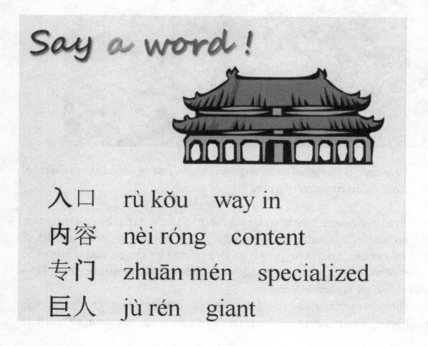

Say a word !

入口	rù kǒu	way in
内容	nèi róng	content
专门	zhuān mén	specialized
巨人	jù rén	giant

A rammer is designed to strengthen the ground or structure < Cultural Heritage Administration of Korea >

同 (同, tong, same) the upper thing means a rammer that is used to harden the ground by ramming, in the middle is the mouth (口, kou, mouth). A ground rammer needs two people to pick up and hit the ground at the same time. When people ramming the ground, they usually shout together. Thus this character is used as 'same'.

This character is also used to express dancing together. 興 (興, 兴, xing=hsing, excitement) has four hands 𦥑 (共, gong, common; altogether) which mean people together. The middle symbolizes 'ramming the ground together'봉 (同, tong, same). Therefore, this character implies everyone standing up, hand-in-hand, excitedly dancing and singing together.

Pottery showing hand-in-hand dancing scene (Neolithic era) <National Museum of China>

丹 (再, zai, again) The wood pieces are arranged vertically and horizontally. When making furniture or building a house, wood is important material and could be scarce. Timbers were piled up regularly to prevent them from rotting or getting warped.

The sign is used to refer to the meaning of 'again' because the same sized pieces of wood are stacked up repeatedly.

高 (高, gao, tall) There is a tall building above the gate. It is a tall and large gate tower built at the entrance to the castle.

Holding a memorial service at a high house (403-221 BC) <Beijing Capital Museum>

The front gate of a castle (1906) <National Folk Museum of Korea >

 (京, jing, capital) There is a tall pavilion above the top, and a high pile. There is a staircase in the middle. The palace is built on a pedestal that is artificially built up. It means 'capital' with the palace where the king stayed.

Say a word!

同意	tóng yì	agree
高兴	gāo xìng	happy
一共	yí gòng	altogether
再见	zài jiàn	say goodbye
提高	tí gāo	raise
北京	Běi jīng	Beijing

Dishes and food

今 (今, jin, present) There is a lid covering the top of the product and food below. The reason why people cover the lid is to eat it immediately before it cools. So now it means ' now '.

合 (合, he, close; combine) The character shows the lid \of the container, depicting the food together in a bowl and covered it with a lid. It is used as the meaning of 'close' or 'gathering'. '

A plate with a lid on food (14th-19th century) <National Folk Museum of Korea >

Usually white rice is steam-cooked in a pot. The smell of rice being cooked was thought to be the sweetest one in ancient times when food was often scarce. 食 食 (食, shi=shih, eat) combines a bowl of a tall pedestal with rice inside it食, and a cover for the bowl ㅅ. A spoon 𠤎 (匕, chi, spoon) is added later, and this symbol came to mean "eat".

Various bowls containing foods. Ancient people used tall vessels to offer sacrifices to God (1st century BC – 7th century AD) < Gyungju National Museum of Korea >

Vessel with a lid (13ᵗʰ century-11ᵗʰ century BC) ‹Yinxu Museum›

香 (香, xiang=hsiang, fragrant) is a combination of a rice plant 禾 (禾, he, standing grain; rice) and a mouth chewing something 甘. It means someone is eating boiled rice. Because the smell was very delicious, it came to mean "fragrant" or "delicious" in the present times.

Wine for sacred ceremony

Grain is used to make alcohol. By different methods such as fermentation or distillation, alcoholic beverages are made. In ancient times, when grain was scarce, only the rich could afford such a luxury.

酒 (酒, jiu, alcoholic drink) means alcoholic drink. This character is a combination of the one that signifies water 水 (水, shui, water) and a pot 酉 to hold the water. Wine/alcoholic beverages were considered to be sacred, so they were used mostly for religious ceremonies or special festivities.

Eggshell-thin black pottery goblet (Neolithic Age) <National Museum of China>

Say a word!

今天	jīn tiān	today
合适	hé shì	appropriate
零食	líng shí	snack
汤匙	tāng chí	soupspoon
香肠	xiāng cháng	sausage
啤酒	pí jiǔ	beer

Weaving cloth

經 (經, 经, jing, pass; channel) There is a thread 糸 on the left. On the right, there are many strands of the thread hanging on the tree 巛, and there is a big loom underneath 工 for weaving. When threads are woven together, then it becomes a fabric. It is now used to mean a 'pass', or 'economy'.

布 (布, bu, cloth) A hand takes a long tool 丆, and the fabric is rolled up 巾. Someone is flattening a piece of cloth with a bat. It is used as the meaning of 'fabric' and 'flatten'.

市 (市, shi, city; market) This character meant 'to stop' 止 (zhi=chih, stop). Below is the roll of cloth, for making clothes. Textiles were an important trading item. This cloth is sold in specific locations, at a 'market' or in a 'city'. Looking at the character 衣 (衣, yi, clothing) which means a garment, we can easily discern two sleeves on both sides. One side of the collar is folded over the other. This character is applied in other characters. For example, 依 (依, yi, to depend on) is a combination of a garment (衣, yi) and a person 亻 who is wearing the garment. He needs to protect himself from the wind, sun, and cold with clothes. Clothes were precious and people treasured their clothes. Therefore, the symbol evolved to "to depend on".

The women are weaving. (18th century) ‹National Museum of Korea ›

Bronze container depicting a weaving scene (206 BC – AD 8) <National Museum of China>

Putting a piece of cloth on the stone tablet, women are beating it with a bat to flatten a cloth (14th-19th century)

<National Folk Museum of Korea >

A garment with a tail

尾 (尾, wei, tail) combines a person 尸 and some sort of ornament 毛 (毛, mao, hair; fur) behind him. A person has something hanging behind him. Now this symbol means "tail".

Even in the present times, there are nomadic tribes. Some of these people live in hot climates. They usually wear simple coverings made out of leaves. Such covering looks like a tail from the back. In the olden days, China was warmer than today, and people who lived in the middle and southern areas of China could have worn such simple clothing.

Say a word!

已经	yǐjīng	already
分布	fēn bù	distribute
超市	chāo shì	supermarket
衣服	yī fu	clothes
依靠	yī kào	rely on
毛巾	máo jīn	towel

5. Everyday Activities

Going Out

The upper part of 𝖀 (出, chu, go out) describes a foot (or foot print) with tows upside↟, and the lower part means the entrance of a cave or a hut ᴜ. It literally shows a man leaving and going outside. Similarly 𝕆 (去, qu=Ch'ü, go) depicts a man 大 leaving an exit U and going somewhere.

In some characters in Hanzi, meaning someone coming in or going out, one will find the symbol of foot. For example, the character which means to be "stable in the house" is like this: 𝙸 (定, ding, stable). Ⴖ is a house, — is a final destination, 𝘞 is a foot which means 'to stop'. Therefore, the character means that someone arrives home and rests.

How should one express walking? In Hanzi, "walking" is symbolized by two foot prints ↟ 𝘞 (步, bu, step). This character shows one right foot↟ followed by a left foot ↟, going forward.

Roads in four directions

Where the main roads meet, that's most likely to be a busy place. There will be lots of markets at such a crossroad. 𝘬 (行, xing=Hsing, walk) means an open crossroad in four directions. Since there were many shops around, this word 行 also means "shop" or "job" as well as "walk".

Sit down and rest under the trees

How can you describe sitting? 交 (交, jiao, hand over; cross). The man is sitting cross-legged. The bottom part is the cross of the legs sitting on the floor instead of on the chair. It develops into the meaning of 'society (dating)' and 'give-and-take'.

A man sitting cross-legged (1915) <National Museum of Korea >

After walking and running, one would feel tired and thirsty and want to rest under the cool shade of a tree. 休 (休, xiu=hsiu, rest) is the description of a person 人 (人, ren, human) resting under a tree 木 (木, mu, tree).

Bathing in a big tub

The people of the Shang Dynasty preferred the color white, which was understood as a very clean. They liked to keep their clothes and bodies clean also.

(浴, yu=yǜ, bath) shows a man ⸌ inside a big tub ⸜ cleaning himself with water ⁖. The tub is similar to the tall pots used for the ceremonies. So we can assume that the ancient people washed themselves before the important ceremonies, especially for the gods.

Say a word !

出租车　chū zū chē　taxi
去年　qù nián　last year
一定　yí dìng　definitely
跑步　pǎo bù　run
自行车　zì xíng chē　bicycle
交通　jiāo tōng　traffic
休息　xiū xi　rest

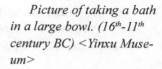

Picture of taking a bath in a large bowl. (16ᵗʰ-11ᵗʰ century BC) <Yinxu Museum>

浴

A big stone bathtub (5ᵗʰ–6ᵗʰ century) < Buyeo National Museum of Korea >

Tattoos

Ancient Chinese, Japanese and Koreans had tattoos. Today, new technology and medicine allow people to get tattoos without much pain. However, being tattooed used to require great tolerance to endure the pain. In the lower part of 克 (克, ke=k'e, restrain), there is a profile of a man ⼫ whose arm is on his hips and emphasizing his shoulders (肩, jian=chien, shoulder). Then, what does the top part 凵 signify?

This symbol has meanings such as tolerance, restraint, defiance, and etc. So we can interpret this character as someone being tattooed in great pain. He is screaming because of the pain with his mouth open and tongue rolled out: 凵

Listen, laugh or cry

𝄞 (听, ting, hear) shows a mouth ⌣ and an ear 𝄢 (耳, er, ear). It is a scene of the loud sound, and listening to the sound. This character used to mean "to laugh with mouth open" before. But now this symbol is used for "listening" instead of the old symbol 聽 (ting, hear) which is too complicated for a common word.

笑 (笑, xiao=Hsiao, laugh) Above are bamboo tree's leaves ⺮, and a person is laughing loudly with his neck bent backward 夭.

A man with tattoo on his shoulder (13th century-11th century BC) <Yinxu Museum>

When the wind blows, the leaves clash in the bamboo forests, rustling and rattling loudly. This character compares the sound of bamboo leaves to people laughing loudly.

Say a word!

淋浴	lín yù	take a shower
克服	kè fú	overcome
打听	dǎ ting	ask about
开玩笑	kāi wán xiào	joke

Picture of Bamboo tree (16th century) <National Museum of Korea >

音 (音, yin, sound) means a knife 辛 (辛, xin=hsin, hot in taste; hard) and a mouth ᴗbeneath it. We can see in the mouth, there is one more line compare to a typical mouth ᴗ;

it seems to describe screaming.

Sword used for cutting sacrifices (13ᵗʰ century-11ᵗʰ century BC) <Yinxu Museum>

This character is now used to mean something good, such as "music", but in the beginning its meaning was not positive. Because there is a "knife" 辛 (辛, xin=hsin, hot in taste; hard) in the picture, it conveys some kind of punishment given with the knife. That is to say, this character suggests a man screaming because he is punished by a knife.

Figurines of women playing musical instrument (left, middle) and Standing Lady (right) (AD 581–618) <Shanghai Museum>

Think and love

(心, xin=hsin, heart) It's a heart and a blood vessel leading to the heart. Ancient people thought that people's minds or emotions were born in the heart. Therefore, it is used as the meaning of 'mind'.

(思, si=ssu, think) describes a head with a knot which has a complex thought (x). There is a heart which means emotions in below the character. The ancients believed that human emotions came from the heart, and complex and logical thoughts come from head. This character is a combination of thoughts and emotions that have mixed feelings of mind and soul.

(愛, 爱, ai, love) A person stands tall, with his/her mouth widely opened 几, breathing long (like Yawning) with heart ∽ (心) in it, and with a foot down to the designated place ⊀ (夂) below. It describes one's mind heartily heads to one's loved one.

Say a word !

音乐　yīn yuè　music
辛苦　xīn kǔ　laborious
放心　fàng xīn　set one's mind
　　　　　　　　at rest
意思　yì si　meaning
爱好　ài hào　hobby

6. KNOWLEDGE & LEARNING

Book/ Volume

Paper was invented by a Chinese person named Cai Lun (Ts'ai Lun) in 105 BC. Before then, Chinese used bones of animals or wooden blocks to write on.

冊 (册, ce=Ts'e, volume; book) is a packet of slats of wood or bamboo tied together with twine. Writers could inscribe or etch writings on them. Bamboo plants provided good materials to etch/inscribe words, and this technology was used as early as 3000 years ago.

. 冊 shows how bamboo was used to write on, and then the pieces were tied together.

A book of thin slices of bamboo and a string for binding it (14ᵗʰ-19ᵗʰ century) <National Folk Museum of Korea >

Woman writing with a brush pen (18ᵗʰ–19ᵗʰ century) <National Museum of Korea >

In modern China, this is the character that is used to signify reading a book: 書 (書, 书, shu, book) On the top there is a hand 聿, and underneath the character is the bottom of the tree 十 (本, ben, root). Like the stump of a tree, a person holds a long, stubby pen tool. Below is a fire 灬 (火, huo, fire) burning for the ancestral rite, and a mouth that means words ⊖ at the rite. This character describes someone recording the words of various people performing at the memorial service. It is now used to mean a book.

論 (論, 论, lun, essay; discuss) The left symbolizes a forthright statement like a spear 言 (言, yan, speak). Upper right corner is a roof or lid ∧ that collects something in it. And there are wood pieces with various records tied up together 冊. The ancients have written a lot of records on bamboo sticks, and they discuss together whether these records are right or wrong. Therefore, this character has become to mean logical theory or a rational discussion.

Say a word !

注册　zhù cè　enroll
图书馆　tú shū guǎn　library
本来　běn lái　original
火车　huǒ chē　train
讨论　tǎo lùn　discuss
语言　yǔ yán　language

Tossing four sticks to tell a fortune

A long time ago, there were various types of divinations in the East, and people used a variety of tools for them.

斅 (教, 教, jiao, teach) is combination of four sticks crossed with each other ✕, and a child♀, hand holding a rod for spanking⚏. This scene shows someone teaching divination using four sticks. Each stick has two sides (front and back) which can make different formations when people throw them on the ground, and fortunes are told depending on their arrangements.

學 (學, 学, xue=hsüueh, study) Also, in this word, you can see two hands holding something ᵗ ᶴand four sticks to tell fortunes ✕. Add the symbol for 'six' 冂 (六, liu, six) which means the number of Changes, or Universe, and a child ♀. All combined, the word shows a scene of a person learning how to tell fortunes by using sticks. This kind of tradition still remains in some parts of Koreans and native Americans. The process of this divination was complex, and people had to learn (學, 学, xue, study) or teach (敎, 教, jiao, teach) the way to practice.

Primitive counting sticks made of wood used to tell fortunes or calculate (14ᵗʰ-19ᵗʰ century) <National Museum of Korea >

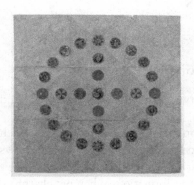

A Korean traditional game playing with four sticks originated in fortunetelling of the year. The author's thesis demonstrating that this game is closely related to 學 (学, xue, study) was accepted in Chinese University (2013). Some American natives also have such a game. <Korean Folk Village>

筭 (算, suan, calculate) Here we see a bamboo tree above, an abacus in the middle, and two hands on the bottom. It describes a person calculating with an abacus that is made of a bamboo.

An abacus, or traditional manual calculator (14ᵗʰ-19ᵗʰ century)
<National Museum of Korea >

Five elements of the universe

The ancient Chinese considered that there were five essential elements in the universe: Water (水, shui), Fire (火, huo), Wood (木, mu), Iron (金, jin), and Earth (土, tu). The five main elements interact and create each other or restrain each other. For example, the tree burns and creates fire which burns down to ashes and becomes earth (soil). Water restrains fire and fire can melt metal.

Ⅹ (五, wu, five) contains such philosophical meanings. The top line means sky 一, the bottom line is earth 一, and the middle Ⅹshows how the "five elements" cross and interact with each other.

7. Money & Partying

Seashells as currency

The Shang Dynasty was established in a location far away from the sea, so it was difficult to get seashells. Yet very beautiful round seashells are found in the Shang Dynasty tombs. Such precious shells were used as currency. In Hanzi=tzu, many words and symbols refer to seashells.

Several words are related to the seashell. For example, 得 (得, de, get) shows hand bending a finger 寸 (寸, cun=ts'un, a small unit of length) to pick up a seashell 貝 (贝, bei, shellfish, the original type is 貝) on the road 行. (行, xing=hsing, walk). It literally means "walking down to the road and picking up a seashell by chance".

The earliest coinage in the world: Seashell (1) used as money from the Stone Age in ancient China. These coins were also made of bone (2), ceramic (3), bronze (4), and gold (5). <Liaoning Provincial Museum>

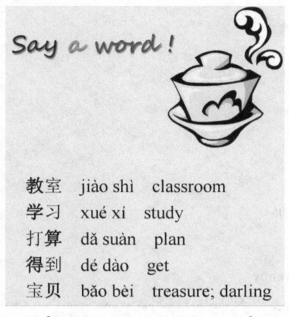

Say a word!

教室	jiào shì	classroom
学习	xué xí	study
打算	dǎ suàn	plan
得到	dé dào	get
宝贝	bǎo bèi	treasure; darling

Making ornaments or money with seashells

The ancient Chinese used seashells not just for currency, but also to wear around the neck as an ornament. 玨 (朋, peng=p'eng, friend) shows two lines of seashells. People used to carry seashells strung together like these because they were esier to carry that way. The appearance of two lines side by side seem like friends, leading this word to mean "friend".

Seashell coins

買 (買, 买, mai, buy) is a combination of a net 网 (网, wang, net) and a seashell 貝. A net is a useful tool for gathering things, and seashells mean money. Therefore, this signifies a scene where a person is purchasing something sold in a net and is paying with seashells.

價 (價, 价, jia, price) On the left is a man, on the right is a lid 襾 of a bowl filled with goods, and a seashell — which means money — below the character. People are selling and buying, haggling over the price.

Precious shiny particles in the soil

金 (金, jin, gold; metal) has a lid covering the top of the object and something under it 今 (今, jin, now), and a soil beneath it 土 (土, tu, soil), and some points dotted around them 丷. As a whole, this character means gathering the shiny particles that are contained in the soil. It originally meant various metals contained in the soil, but later it came to mean gold.

Shellfish currency and a line (11ᵗʰ century – 10ᵗʰ century BC) <Beijing Capital Museum>

鏺 (錢, 钱, qian=Ch'ien, money) The left means metal particles shining in the soil 金, and on the right there are metal spears 戔 stacked up. In old times, there was a thin coin that looked like a spear. People bundled up the spears like coins with a string. Now it means 'money'.

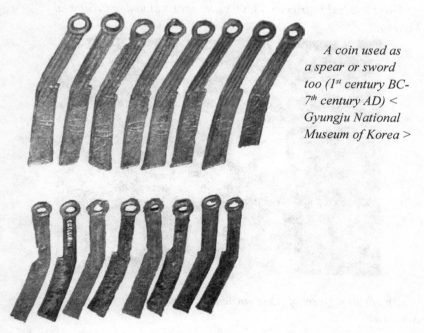

A coin used as a spear or sword too (1ˢᵗ century BC– 7ᵗʰ century AD) < Gyungju National Museum of Korea >

Playing music

In ancient China, people enjoyed music created on various instruments. 殸閣 (聲, 声, sheng, sound) is a character combination which shows a musical instrument 𠂊 (石, shi, stone) that is made by a flat stone, an ear 𠂤 (耳, er, ear), a mouth which is singing ㅂ, a bow to play the instrument𝟙, and a hand 𝟡 which is holding the bow. All together, it shows someone playing a stone instrument similar to the one shown below. Later the meaning of the word evolved to mean "sound".

Stone musical instrument (3300 years ago) <Liaoning Provincial Museum>

An advanced form of stone musical instrument <Min-Tai Affinity Museum>

Women playing on musical instruments made of stone and bronze (406-221 BC) <Shanghai Museum>

Bells (9ᵗʰ century BC) <Shanghai Museum>

Dancing

How did the ancient East Asians dance? 舛 舞 (舞, wu, dance) symbolizes a person holding some kind of ivy or ornament and waving it. The ornaments were also used to embellish war drums, bells, or carriages. Because of their colors and fluttering texture, the ornaments catch your eye. 舛

Previous page: *In the royal ancestral memorial rites held by the designated authorities, the officials of the royal ancestral memorial altar held the ornaments in both hands. < Lee Royal Family Association, Korea >*

Painted pottery dancer (East Han Dynasty AD 25-220) <National Museum of China>

Say a word !

朋友	péng you	friend
买单	mǎi dān	bill
价格	jià gé	price
现金	xiàn jīn	cash
零钱	líng qián	small change
声音	shēng yīn	voice; sound
跳舞	tiào wǔ	dance

8. WAR

Making weapons

There were many wars and battles during the Shang Dynasty (16th century – 11th century BC). Thus, people often came up with ideas for weapons and for battle strategies when fighting with neighboring countries.

兵 (兵, bing, arms) contains a shape of an axe 斤 (斤, jin, a unit of weight; original shape is 𠂤, left is a tree caved in, right is an ax) and two hands in a clasped 廾. It is an image of someone wielding an axe.

Axe of Shang Dynasty (16th century-11th century BC) <Yinxu Museum>

This axe is also a part of another word 新 (新, xin=hsin, new). This word has a pointy blade ⟂and a tree ✳ (木, mu, tree) beneath it, and an axe cutting the tree 斤 (斤, jin, a unit of weight). Something cut by an axe roughly was an unit of weight before, and now this unit is used as an important unit of weight (500g).

Arms of Shang Dynasty (16ᵗʰ century-11ᵗʰ century BC) <Yinxu Museum>

All together, 新 (新, xin=hsin, new) means "spear, tree, axe". In other words, the word shows a scene of making a new spear by using an axe and a tree. So, now it came to mean "new".

The Commander readies the army

Army commanders have to check many things constantly, such as weapons, supplies, food, and the morale. 師 (師, 师, shi=shih, teacher) shows a small hill ⻖ and the action of walking around the hill repeatedly 帀 (還, 还, huan;hai, return; still).

Bronze helmet of Shang Dynasty (16th century-11th century BC) <Yinxu Museum>

A commander is a leader who would march his army around the small hill which was often used as a fortress. A leader of an army was required to look all around carefully and to be a role model. The same role of being a leader in the class is the teacher. The word for "commander" came to mean "teacher" in modern days.

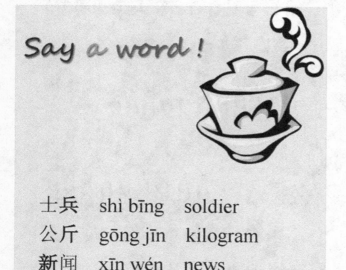

Say a word !

士兵	shì bīng	soldier
公斤	gōng jīn	kilogram
新闻	xīn wén	news
老师	lǎo shī	teacher
还是	hái shi	still

Recruiting soldiers for justice

The purpose of war was said to be to achieve God's will. If a country goes against God's will, surrounding nations gather power to prepare for war against that country.

莪 (我, wo, I; me) The left side is a flag that is divided into three strands. 手

And the right- side is a long spear 戈. In ancient times, when war broke out, a flag was hung on the long spear. People who saw the flag joined the war. The People who gathered under one flag was same minded soldiers. Thus, this character became to mean 'our side', 'I (me) '.

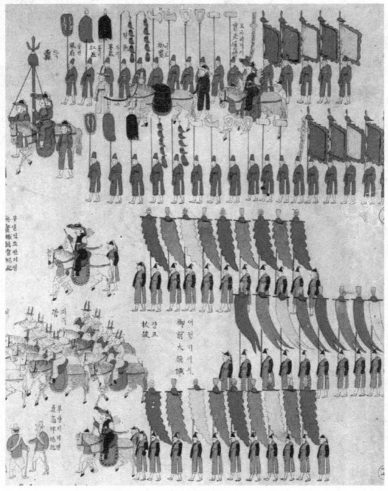

Soldiers carrying flags in a long spear. (14ᵗʰ-19ᵗʰ century, printed in 1926) <National Museum of Korea >

After collecting the soldiers, they offered sacrifices to God. 羛 (義, 义, yi, righteousness) Above means lamb 羊 (羊, yang, sheep).

Stone ram which stood in front of a tomb or a building. It played a role in defeating evil. <National Folk Museum of Korea >

Below is a flag on the spear 栽 (我, wo, I; me) symbolizing the soldiers who have the same mind. Sheep is a sacred offering to God. The purpose of serving sacrifices to God before war is to verify their justice.

Attack at a "timely opportunity"

When the weather becomes warm, it is convenient to wage war against another country. Therefore, the ancient Chinese used to call "a month favorable to invade" as "Zheng Yue (=Cheng Yüeh), 正月 ", which means lunar month of January in East Asia. "Zheng Yue" falls usually is in Feburary in the standard calendar year. 正 (正, zheng, correct) describes a person approaching a village or a fortress. It has 口 on top, which implies the fences or the walls around a village or a fortress, and there is a character signifying foot ∀ under the word.

In the present time, this word means "correct". But before then, it meant "to attack". In the past, the purpose of the war was to correct the fault of some area. Therefore this character came to mean 'right', 'exact'.

Bronze WeaGrappling Hook used when attack the castle. (16th century-11th century BC) <Yinxu Museum>

昰 (是, shi, be; right) the sun ⊖ rises above the horizon, and a foot (that stands for walking) goes forward 疋 (正, zheng, correct). The sun was like a deity. Thus, this character means to do the 'right' thing. Now it is used as 'yes', 'be'.

Travel to war

The word "travel" originates from the scene of marching in line: 㫃旒 (旅, lü, travel). A flag and two people marching 从 (從, 从, cong=ts'ung, follow). In other words, it symbolizes people following the flag and marching.

At that time, 500 soldiers were called up 旅 (lü) for war. Therefore this character implies about 500 people following a military flag.

Soldiers marching with flags (14th-19th century) <National Museum of Korea >

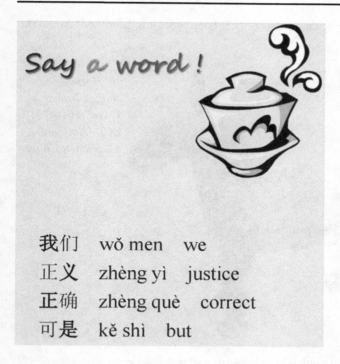

我们　wǒ men　we
正义　zhèng yì　justice
正确　zhèng què　correct
可是　kě shì　but

Picture of marching (8th century-3th century BC) <Beijing Capital Museum>

Nowadays, this word means "travel". However, back when the word was first used, leisurely travel or travelling as a form of entertainment was rare. There were too many costs, and dangers and threats outside of one's home. However, going somewhere with a mission, such as to invade another tribe, was common.

馬 (馬, 马, ma, horse) describes a horse with big head and shows the horse's mane.

Horse-shaped Bronze Vessel (1046-771 BC) <National Museum of China>

車 (車, 车, che, vehicle) is a horse-drawn war wagon.

Originally such wagons had two wheels, but for simplicity's sake the character depicts just one wheel, in the middle.

Carriage buried with a horse driver (13th century-11th century BC) <Yinxu Museum>

Carriage buried with horses (13th century-11th century BC). When the king of the Shang Dynasty died, many servants and horses were killed and buried together. <Yinxu Museum>

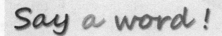

旅游	lǚ yóu	tour
顺从	shùn cóng	obey
马上	mǎ shàng	right away
堵车	dǔ chē	traffic jam

Battle drum

To communicate and give orders to soldiers, a loud signal system was needed. A drum was a useful instrument to achieve such an important goal. Many soldiers moved following the orders given by the drum beats.

中 (中, zhong, center) shows a long pole and some fluttering pennants attached to it. And in the middle there is a square board.

On a bronze plaque from 403 - 221 BC, there is a picture of a soldier beating the drum in a scene of a war. Drums were hung on the 'middle' of a pole. The depiction of the battle drum came to mean center 中 (zhong, center) in present times.

When a battle began, the drums were used to lift the morale of the soldiers.

Warrior beating a drum (403-221 BC) <Beijing Capital Museum>

In the word 鼓 (鼓, gu, drum, rouse) you can also see a drum on the left 壴 and on a right hand, beating the drum vigorously 攴 (支, zhi=chih, support).

Bass drum (restoration) (16th century- 11th century BC) <Yinxu Museum>

Shooting arrows

With the sound of the drums, once the battle started, the sky would be covered with flying arrows from both directions. 𡕥 𡈼 (至, zhi=chih, to; till) shows a target ▭ and an arrow coming down 𡗗 (矢). Together, the characters form the word "to get somewhere".

Inlaid picture of bronze wine vessel (5th century-4th century BC) <Shanghai Museum>

Warrior shooting an arrow (AD 618-907) <Xiamen Chinese emigrants Museum>

引 (引, yin, draw) shows an action of drawing an arrow from the bow. There are the bow 弓 (弓) and bowstring Ⅰ. Since it was not easy to make a firm bowstring back then, the string was not attached to the bow all the time. The bow with the string unfastened looks like this: 弓 弓 (gong, bow).

Injury in battle

的 (的, de, di, target) On the left side is the white target
白 (白, bai, white), and the right is a bow with an arrow 弓.
Someone shoots the arrow at the white target.

Later on, the right side of the symbol was replaced by a ladle (勺) instead of a bow, meaning 'target'.

People hunting birds with arrow (5th century-4th century BC) <Shanghai Museum>

Repair bow and arrow, Practice shooting (18th century) <National Museum of Korea >

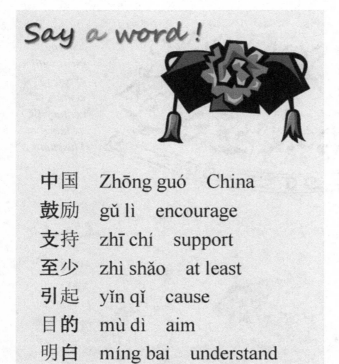

Say a word!

中国	Zhōng guó	China
鼓励	gǔ lì	encourage
支持	zhī chí	support
至少	zhì shǎo	at least
引起	yǐn qǐ	cause
目的	mù dì	aim
明白	míng bai	understand

When enemies are far enough away, soldiers attack with arrows, but when the distance is shorter, they use spears.

武 (武, wu, military) is a combination of a spear 戈 (戈) and a foot 止. It implies a person running with his spear.

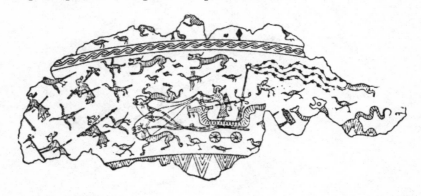

Military march, picture of bronze vessel (403-221 BC) <Beijing Capital Museum>

Broken blade

Since the sword is crucial in protecting oneself during battle, when the blade is broken, one may well be doomed. Having a strong blade is a matter of life and death.

Here is a sword: 匕 (刀, dao, sword).

By contrast, 匕 (亡, wang, flee; lose) shows a sword whose blade is blunt or cut off. In other words, the sharp part of the blade was destroyed and became flat.

Bronze sword (16th century- 11th century BC) <Yinxu Museum>

Defeated side; Broken bronze plate

敗 (敗, 败, bai, defeat) shows a combination of a seashell which was used as a currency 貝 , and on the right of the character is a hand holding a stick 攵, depicting the action of breaking the seashell with a weapon.

Previous page: *Bronze vessels were the symbol of the divine right of kings in ancient China. (16th century- 11th century BC) <Yinxu Museum>*

The seashell 貝 sometimes also signifies a precious bronze ceremonial vessel that symbolizes the spiritual importance and the power of a king. Therefore, the action of wrecking the ceremonial plate means a serious failure or the defeat of the country.

9. DEATH

Retired, sick, dying

免 (免, mian=mien, exempt)The top is a hat decorated with feathers or animal horns免, and there is a person below 儿. This represents the hat used by officials. Taking off this hat means leaving office. This character depicts an officer taking retiring frm work and stepping down from his office. It is used with a meaning of ' to escape ' and ' to avoid '.

If the sun 日 (ri, sun) isadded to this character, it means 'evening' 晚 (wan, evening; late). That is, the sun has done his duty an is going away.

Officials marching to the tomb of the King, wearing hats decorated with standing feathers (printed in 1926) < National Palace Museum of Korea >

疒 (病, bing, disease; sickness) depicts an old person 老 (老, lao, old) lying in bed 爿 with a pillow—. It shows that the old person is ailing.

133

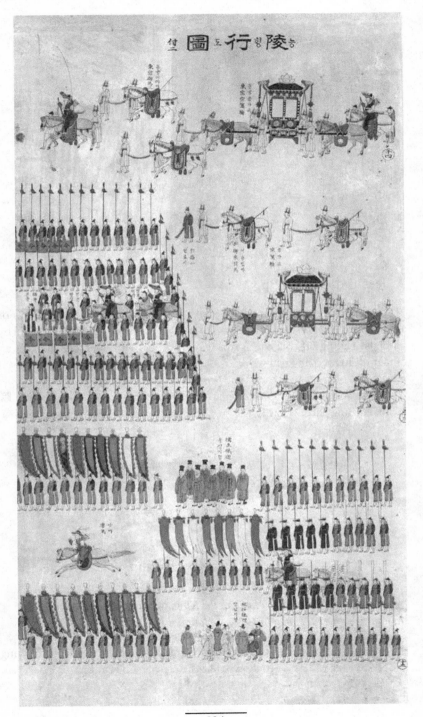

//

Wooden bed (14th-19th century) <National Folk Museum of Korea >

Death

What was the funeral like 3000 years ago? In ancient times, only high class people were able to use coffins. 朋 (死, si=ssu, death) implies a kneeling person 人, and to his left are the bones 歺 (骨, gu, bone). Back then, when a person died, they would take the corpse into the open field for some time and then come back to collect the bones. The picture shows a man mourning before the bones of a dead one.

In ancient China, funerals were considered "bad luck" and when a person died, they took the corpse to a field far away. The ancient book "Zhou Yi" says that:

"The funeral ceremony of olden times consisted of dressing the corpse in thick clothes and covering it with branches and hiding it in a field. It was not a burial and there was not a tombstone."

Say a word!

武术	wǔ shù	martial arts; Wushu
灭亡	miè wáng	destroy
失败	shī bài	fail
免费	miǎn fèi	be free of charge
晚上	wǎn shang	evening
生病	shēng bìng	get sick
死亡	sǐ wáng	die
排骨	pái gǔ	spareribs or spines

PART 3 地 (DI) EARTH

1. FROM WATER TO WATER

Breathing of the earth

When fall came and the dew in the fields would evaporate in the early sunshine, people could often see morning fog. They thought of that morning fog as the breath of the earth.

氣 (氣, 气, qi=ch'i, gas; air) The character shows vapor rising from the earth.

Flowing water looks like this: 水 (水, shui, water). But compared to flowing water, ╵ this character shows stillness.

Later, people added the character symbolizing hot steam coming from rice 米 (米, mi, rice) that is being cooked 氣 (qi=ch'i). But in the 1950s, the simplified Chinese characters policy changed 氣 (qi) to its original form: 气 (qi).

Underworld beneath the spring

泉 (泉, quan=ch'üan, spring) suggests water from a spring 白and flowing downwards through the waterway川. It depicts springwater gushing from the depths. The ancient Chinese thought of life as being like a flowing stream, coming from somewhere and going somewhere unknown. Therefore, they called the place where dead people go a "yellow spring (黃泉)", or "netherworld". They believed that when one died, one would go to underworld beneath the spring.

Beautiful mountain of China (Huang Shan, Anhui Province, China)

Endless river

The Yellow River that flows through China is one of the longest rivers in the world. The river is so long that the ancient Chinese probably thought that it was endless. Therefore, a long river's endless flow came to mean "forever".

永 (永, yong, forever) was created to mean such thoughts.

The character shows a person 亻 (人, ren, human), a road 彳 (行, xing=hsing, line), and a flow of water 丶. It signifies a man swimming in the river: 泳 (泳, yong, swim) or walking next to a river. He would think the river is so long, and the flow of water is endless.

Ancient boat (206 BC - AD 220) <Historical Museum of China>

Vapor floating in the sky

Rain is expressed as ⻗ 雨 (雨, yu=yŭ, rain). It shows raindrops falling from the sky. A cloud is composed of water vapor, and floats in the sky by the wind. 雲 (雲, 云, yun=yün, cloud) means rain 雨, vapor or steam ⚌ on the above, and something whirling ひ beneath it . It describes the cloud whirling in the sky. These characters combined to mean "a cloud which carries rain".

With the implementation of simplified Chinese, now the character 雲 (yun=yün, cloud) has been changed to the simple form 云 (云, yun=yün, cloud), meaning a cloud.

Jade Dragon (4700-2900 BC) Chinese proverb says that the dragon walks on the clouds. <National Museum of China>

天气　　tiān qì　　weather

米饭　　mǐ fàn　　cooked rice

永远　　yǒng yuǎn　　eternally

游泳　　yóu yǒng　　swim

下雨　　xià yǔ　　rain

2. FARM

Farming the lands

田 (田, tian=t'ien, field) depicts farmland divided into four areas. In olden times, the fields were not clearly divided to separate farmlands and hunting fields. Farmland was an area where one could hunt as well as farm.

Stone tools in shape of shovels (Neolithic Age) <Liaoning Provincial Museum>

The symbol for boundary is this: 畍 (界, jie, boundary). The upper part of the symbol is a field 田 (田, tian=t'ien, field) and the left shows a person 人 (人, ren, human) between the two things 𝕀 (介, jie, be situated between). He is now deciding the exact borders of the fields.

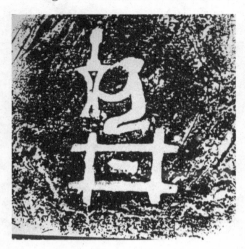

A person is holding a drink next to the well. (1600 to 1046 BC) <Beijing Capital Museum>

During the Shang Dynasty (1, 600 to 1, 046 BC), the fields were divided in the shape of a well 井 (井, jing, well). Eight households got a part of eight outside divisions, and the middle part of this field 井 was for co-cultivation.

3. Fun with Animals

Cow with horns

角角 (角, jiao, horn) is a sharp horn of an animal. Animals' horns were a useful material, especially cow horns which are strong, sturdy and have pretty colors. Therefore people used them to decorate furniture, toys, or even musical instruments.

Horn glass (1ˢᵗ century BC-7ᵗʰ century) < Gyungju National Museum of Korea >

However, it was not easy to take the horn from a cow. In order to get the horn, first, the people heated the horn to make it softer and then used a knife to cut it off from the cow.

Bronze cow-shaped ceremonial bowl (16ᵗʰ century-11ᵗʰ century BC) <Yinxu Museum>

The character 解 (解, jie, separate) describes such works. It is composed of a man holding a horn of a cow 牛 (牛, niu, cow), with a knife 刀 (刀, dao, knife).

Because it took a lot of strength and manpower, when a man had successfully done the work, he felt he had "solved" a problem. Thus, now this character 解 (jie) means not only "to separate", but also "to solve" or "to dissolve".

Cow pulling wagon (550~577) <National Museum of China>

Elephant with decorations

Cup made of ivory elephant tusks (left), Jade elephant (right) (13th century-11th century BC). In ancient China, elephants and alligators existed in the areas with warm climates. <Yinxu Museum>

Thousands years ago, China's weather was warmer than today. So, big fish and big animals lived around the Yellow River, including the elephant. The elephant was drawn like this: But for the convenience of writing, the character was flipped vertically (象, xiang=hsiang, elephant). It shows the characteristics of the elephant quite clearly, especially the elephant's big head, protruding long nose and long ears.

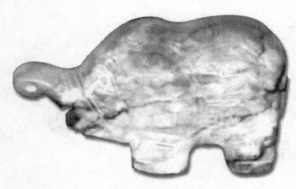

People used to decorate elephants just as current Southeast Asian people adorn elephants today. Therefore, now this character 象 (x i a n g = h s i a n g, elephant) also comes to mean "to decorate, to copy, to resemble".

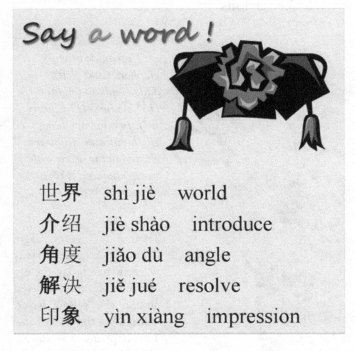

Say a word !

世界　shì jiè　world
介绍　jiè shào　introduce
角度　jiǎo dù　angle
解决　jiě jué　resolve
印象　yìn xiàng　impression

Human supports elephant

爲 (爲, 为, wei, support; do) shows that elephants were very well-cared for. This character means "to support" or "for someone". The top part is a hand 爪, and the bottom part is an elephant 象 (象, xiang=hsiang). In other words, someone is doing something for the elephant such as giving it food or decorating it.

Gold ornament in the shape of a deer and a tiger (403-221 BC)
<Liaoning Provincial Museum>

Crazy dog

Since vaccines were not discovered yet, there were many dogs with rabies. The English expression "rabid dog" had a strong meaning back in those times. Dogs that had rabies went mad and bit people and showed ferocity. People had to be very careful not to be bitten by mad dogs. The character 𤽀 狂 (狂, kuang, mad) describes this kind of situation. The left part of this character means a foot ⾜ (止, zhi=chih, stop) on a high mound ⼟ (土, tu, soil). On the right, there is a dog犭. In other words, it depicts someone stopped on a high place and a dog beneath it barking ferociously.

Pottery dog (AD 265-420) <Beijing Capital Museum>

Is a dragon an alligator or a bear?

There used to be the alligators in China,. 𤣥 (龍, 龙, long, dragon) depicts a big animal with big mouth (𠂤) and a long tail (𠃊). This animal could be an alligator or a big snake whose teeth are like spears𨑃 (辛, xin=hsin, hot; bitter). Ancient Hanzi books explain that "a Dragon has scales and is the king of animals." Therefore alligators that look like they have thick scales could be understood to be Dragons. Dragon is considered a symbol of China. The Chinese refer to themselves as "the descendants of the Dragon."

Jade dragon (13ᵗʰ century-11ᵗʰ century BC) <National Museum of China>

A sculpture of a dragon (206 BC-AD220) <Shanghai Museum>

On the other hand, in northeastern China, many excavations have resulted in the discovery of jade ornaments, and many dragon ornaments also resemble bears. Interestingly, some scholars even suggest the resemblance to pigs as well. Now the jade ornaments are seen as "bear-dragons." In other words, it is still not definite whether the jade dragon ornaments are also alligators or bears.

Dragon-shaped Jade ornaments (13th century-11th century BC) It is discussed recently in Chinese academia that the shapers are developed from bear shapes. <Yinxu Museum>

Crouching owl

舊 (舊, 旧, jiu, past) shows an owl on the top 萑 and its claws 臼. It used to mean birds like owls, but now it came to mean "old" or "worn."

Owls do not hunt during the day like other birds. Owls are nocturnal. So during the day an owl usually sits still.

Owl sitting still < Cultural Heritage Administration of Korea >

The ancient people thought owls were crouching still and sleeping. Therefore, the character came to mean "old" and "worn" as well.

Jade shaped Bird (13ᵗʰ century-11ᵗʰ century BC) Birds were considered as messengers of God in Ancient china. <Yinxu Museum>

The Stork observes

觀 (觀, 观, guan, observe) This symbol is composed of a bird with a mouth on each side and a person watching it carefully (見, 见, jian=chien, see; meet with). It shows a bird crying or singing loudly and looking around carefully. Such a bird is a stork or crane. The character has also come to mean "to observe, to enjoy the scenary."

Pictures of pine and crane. (19th-early 20ᵗʰ centtury) < National Palace Museum of Korea >

This bird is different from the symbol which describes bird in general 鳳 (鳥, 鸟, niao, bird).

Duck-Shaped Bronze wine vessel (1046-771 B.C) <National Museum of China>

Phoenix, a bird of Wind (13th century-11th century BC) <Yinxu Museum>

Worms and bugs

蟲 (蟲, 虫, chong, insect) It features a large group of worms that have sharp heads and crawling bodies. Some worms, like caterpillars, have a poisonous sting, so that it is pointed with a sharp prick as it stings like a snake.

強 (强, qiang, strong) The left side is the bow弓, and the upper right is the horn of the insect that looks like a mouth 𠃊, and an insect 虫 underneath that. It is a stag beetle with arched horns like a bow. Stag beetles are strong and powerful. One bite brings a great deal of pain to a person.

It is therefore used as ' strong '.

Stag beetles with bow-like horn <The Academy of Korean Studies>

凩 (風, 风, feng, wind) ∩ means a house or a shelter from the sun, and 𧈧 is a stinging worm. In the winter, a cold wind blows in through the cracks of the house, just like a venomous worm's sting; therefore, this character became to mean a 'wind'.

Because the wind comes from the outside, it also refers to the customs and scenery of other regions and places.

Say a word!

为什么　wèi shén me　why

疯狂　fēng kuáng　crazy

参观　cān guān　tour

坚强　jiān qiáng　strong

风俗　fēng sú　custom

Scorpions on a stick

龝 (萬, 万, wan, ten thousand) is the shape of scorpion 𧊙. The tail of this character shows a hook with three swords (trident): 九 (九, jiu, nine). In ancient times, people often ate large numbers of scorpions that they cooked, skewered on a stick. Now it means the number 10,000. This could be also due to scorpion's characteristics of living in groups and laying many eggs.

Scorpions live in groups. Thailand

Since usually many scorpions are skewered at one time, the word came to mean 'many'.

Trident (14th-19th century) <National Museum of Korea >

4. HUNTING

Using stones to hunt

ᛘ單 (單,单, dan, single) portrays a tool used for hunting In ancient times. There are two pebbles above ₀ ₀, and underneath the pebbles there are lines in the shape of the letter V (Υ). This is an ancient form of a stone slingshot for shooting a stone.

The middle character ⊕ (田, tian=t'ien, field) means "field". So this character implies that one is hunting in the wide field with the slingshot.

A slingshot can only shoot one stone at a time. Therefore, a long time later when the stone slingshot disappeared, this character was no longer used to mean a weapon, instead it came to mean "single."

Animal-Shaped Wine Vessel (13ᵗʰ century-11ᵗʰ century BC) <Shanghai Museum>

The Flight of a clever bird

離 (離, 离, li, leave) is composed of a bird 隹 (鳥, 鸟, niao, bird) and a snare 离 (网, wang, net) which can catch the bird. Birds are very perceptive so they fly away quickly even at the slightest hint of someone approaching. Therefore, this Chinese character evolved to mean "to depart" or "to leave".

Eagle-Shaped Pottery vessel (5000-3000 BC) <National Museum of China>

魚 (魚, 鱼, yu=yü, fish) This is a fish figure. The top is the head of the fish, the middle part is a body, and the bottom is the tail fin.

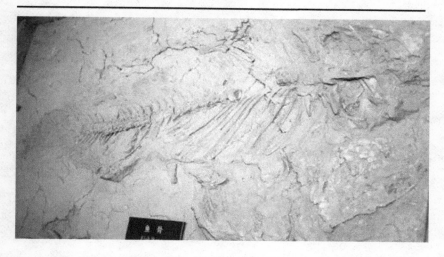

Large fish skeleton. Thousands of years ago, the climate of China was milder than now. Large animals and large fishes could live in China. <Yinxu Museum>

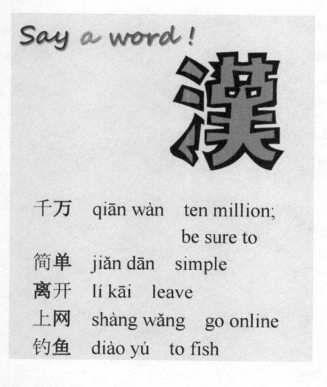

Say a word!

千万	qiān wàn	ten million; be sure to
简单	jiǎn dān	simple
离开	lí kāi	leave
上网	shàng wǎng	go online
钓鱼	diào yú	to fish

5. GRAIN

The smallest grain, millet

八 川 (小, xiao=hsiao, small) means a few small grains. The grains could be millet grains which were consumed in northern ancient China. Millets are one of the tiniest grains. Therefore it came to mean "small".

Grain used in ceremonies

豊 (豊, 丰, feng, abundant) is composed of a ceremonial bowl 豆 (豆, dou, bean) and many pods of beans or ears of grain 丰.

Lacquer dou stemmed vessel (Replica). Hemispherical bowl used for offering beans, grain and fruit (11th century-10th century BC) <Beijing Capital Museum>

Bulrush/ Reed Mace, materials used to make instruments for many purposes.

This Chinese character 豐 (丰, feng, abundant) also means a bulrush or reed mace. These are edible plants which are tall (about four to five feet) and they render their grain for people to eat. The stalks from the plants are also useful in making mats, hats, and baskets. The plants were even used as medicine.

The ceremonial bowl filled with these useful grains evolved to mean "abundant". Also, the character developed to mean ritual, ceremony or manners: 禮 (禮, 礼, li, ceremony; courtesy).

Sacred barley from the heavens

(來, 来, lai, come) This character originally meant barley (麥, 麦, mai, wheat; barley). According to the ancient scripts, this character meant "to receive holy barley." In other words, it meant that heaven (天, tian=t'ien) gave barley to humanity; the sacred barley came from heaven. Therefore the character came to mean "to come."

Ripe Barley

Say a word!

小姐	xiǎo jiě	Miss
丰富	fēng fù	abundant
豆腐	dòu fu	tofu; bean curd
礼貌	lǐ mào	manners
小麦	xiǎo mài	wheat

Writing Exercise - Part 1

天 Tian=T'ien, Heaven

In this section, we learn a bit about calligraphy by looking at a number of characters and learning the sequence of the brush strokes to draw each one.

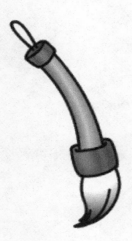

1. THE GOD OF HEAVEN

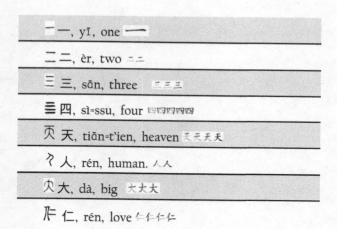

一, yī, one

二, èr, two

三, sān, three

四, sì=ssu, four

天, tiān=t'ien, heaven

人, rén, human.

大, dà, big

仁, rén, love

2. THE KING WHO IS THE AGENT OF HEAVEN

玉 王, wáng, king 王王王王

关 央, yāng, middle 央央央央央

桨 英, yīng, flower 英英英英英英英英

㳒 光, guāng, light 光光光光光光光

黄 黄, huáng, yellow 黄黄黄黄黄黄黄黄黄黄黄

土 土, tǔ, earth 土土土

示 示, shì =shih, show 示示示示示

社 社, shè, society 社社社社社社社

里 里, lǐ, place, inside 里里里里里里里里

田 田, tián =t'ien, field 田田田田田

理 理, lǐ, manage, reason 理理理理理理理理理

王, 玉 yù =yü, jade 玉玉玉玉玉

169

3. Aristocrats Wear Horns

告 告, gào, inform 告告告告告告告

廿 口, kǒu, mouse 口口口

監 监, jiàn =chien, supervise 监监监监监监监监监

鄉 乡, xiāng =hsiang, countryside 乡乡

美 美, měi, beautiful 美美美美美美美美美

羊 羊, yáng, sheep 羊羊羊羊羊羊

4. THE RELIGIOUS CEREMONY WITH RICE, WINE, MEAT AND BLOOD

位, wèi, position; location

立, lì, stand

福, fú, blessing

尊, zūn, respect

寸, cùn=ts'un, unit of length approximately 3cm

祝, zhù, express good wishes

比, bǐ, compare

北, běi, north

肉, ròu, flesh

背, bèi, back

血, xiě =hsieh, blood

益, yì, benefit, increase

173

5. ANIMAL SACRIFICE FOR RELIGIOUS CEREMONIES

物物, wù, thing 物物物物物物物

半牛, niú, cattle 牛牛牛牛

刀刀, dāo, knife 刀刀

多多, duō, many 多多多多多多

有有, yǒu, have 有有有有有有

又, yòu, again 又又

員員, yuán =yüan, member 员员员员员员员

獻献, xiàn, dedicate 献献献献献献献献献

虎虎, hǔ, tiger 虎虎虎虎虎虎虎虎

沉沉, chén, sink 沉沉沉沉沉沉沉

175

6. Messengers Of God: Bronze, And Bones

丙 不, bù, no; not 不不不不

杯 bēi, cup 杯杯杯杯杯杯杯杯

商 否, fǒu, deny 否否否否否否否

畵 禍, 祸, huò, misfortune 祸祸祸祸祸祸祸祸祸祸

7. THE PEOPLE FROM THE SUN AND THE STARS

萅	春, chūn, spring 盂盂吞寿寿寿春春
艸	草, cǎo =ts'ao, grass 艹艹艹艹艹艹芦草草
日	日, rì, sun; day 日日日日
曐	星, xīng =hsing star 星星星星星星星星星
生	生, shēng, to live, life 生生生生生
晶	晶, jīng, brilliant 日日日日日日日日日晶晶晶
七	七, qī =ch'i, seven 七七

WRITING EXERCISE - PART 2

人 Ren, Human

1. PEOPLE

夫, fū, husband 夫夫夫夫

長, 长, zhǎng; cháng, older; long 长长长长

老, lǎo, old 老老老老老老

兒, 儿, ér =erh, child 儿儿

先, xiān =hsien, earlier 先先先先先先

止, zhǐ =chih, stop 止止止止

聖, 圣, shèng, holy; sage 圣圣圣圣圣

耳, ěr, ear 耳耳耳耳耳耳

女, nǚ, woman 女女女

安, ān, peaceful 安安安安安安

入, rù, enter 入入

客, kè =k'e, visitor 客客客客客客客客客

183

2. FAMILY DYNAMICS

祖 祖, zǔ, ancestor 祖祖祖祖祖祖祖祖

且 且, qiě =ch'ieh, and 且且且且且

父 父, fù, father 父父父父

妻 妻, qī =ch'i, wife 妻妻妻妻妻妻妻妻

母 母, mǔ, mother 母母母母母

每 每, měi, every; each 每每每每每每每

海 海, hǎi, sea 海海海海海海海海海海

水 水, shuǐ, water 水水水水

兄 兄, xiōng =hsiung, elder brother 兄兄兄兄兄

弟 弟, dì, younger brother 弟弟弟弟弟弟

孫 孙, sūn, grandchild 孙孙孙孙孙孙

絲 丝, sī =ssu, silk 丝丝丝丝丝丝

身 身, shēn, body 身身身身身身身

育 育, yù =yü, bring up 育育育育育育育

好 好, hǎo, good; love 好好好好好好

185

保 保, bǎo, protect 保保保保保保保保

棄 棄, 弃, qì =ch'i, abandon 弃弃弃弃弃弃弃

其 其, qí =ch'i, that 其其其其其其其其

3. BODY PARTS

面, miàn =mien, face 面面面面面面面面面

目, mù, eye 目目目目

直, zhí =chih, straight 直直直直直直直直

十, shí, ten 十十

看, kàn, see; look at 看看看看看看看看看

手, shǒu, hand 手手手手

见, jiàn =chien, meet with 见见见见

自, zì =tzu, self 自自自自

齿, chǐ =ch'ih, tooth 齿齿齿齿齿齿齿齿齿

右, yòu, right 右右右右右右

左, zuǒ, left 左左左左左左

力, lì, power 力力

男, nán, man 男男男男男男男男

幼, yòu, young; under age 幼幼幼幼幼幼

4. House, Food, and Clothes

人入, rù, enter 入入

內内, nèi, inner 内内内内

門門, 门, mén, door, gate 门门门

工工, gōng, worker 工工工

叵巨, jù =chü, huge 巨巨巨巨

同同, tóng, same 同同同同同

興興, 兴, xìng =hsing, excitement 兴兴兴兴兴兴

共共, gòng, common; altogether 共共共共共

冉再, zài, again 再再再再再再

高高, gāo, tall 高高高高高高高高高

京京, jīng, capital 京京京京京京京京

今今, jīn, present 今今今今

合合, hé, close; combine 合合合合合合

食食, shí =shih, eat 食食食食食食食食

匕匙, chí, spoon 匙匙匙匙匙匙匙匙匙匙

189

香 香, xiāng =hsiang, fragrant	香香香香香香香香香
酒 酒, jiǔ, alcoholic drink	酒酒酒酒酒酒酒酒酒
經 經, 经, jīng, pass; channel	经经经经经经经经经
布 布, bù, cloth	布布布布布布
市 市, shì, city; market	市市市市市市
衣 衣, yī, clothing	衣衣衣衣衣衣
依 依, yī, to depend on	依依依依依依依依
尾 尾, wěi, tail	尾尾尾尾尾尾尾尾
毛 毛, máo, hair; fur	毛毛毛毛

5. Everyday Actions

出, chū, go out 出出出出出
去, qù =ch'ü, go 去去去去去去
定, dìng, stable 定定定定定定定定
步, bù, step 步步步步步步步步
行, xíng =hsing, walk 行行行行行行
交, jiāo, hand over; cross 交交交交交交
休, xiū =hsiu, rest 休休休休休休休
木, mù, tree 木木木木
浴, yù =yü, bath 浴浴浴浴浴浴浴浴浴
克, kè =k'e, restrain 克克克克克克克
听, tīng, hear 听听听听听听听
笑, xiào =hsiao, laugh 笑笑笑笑笑笑笑笑笑
音, yīn, sound 音音音音音音音音
辛, xīn =hsin, hot in taste; hard 辛辛辛辛辛辛辛

191

心, xīn =hsin, heart

思, sī =ssu, think

愛, 爱, ài, love

6. KNOWLEDGE & LEARNING

冊 册, cè =Ts'e, volume; book	册 册 册 册 册
書 書, 书, shū, book	书 书 书 书
本 本, běn, root	本 本 本 本 本
火 火, huǒ, fire	火 火 火 火
論 論, 论, lùn, essay; discuss	论 论 论 论 论 论
言 言, yán, speak	言 言 言 言 言 言 言
教 教, jiāo, teach	教 教 教 教 教 教 教 教 教 教
學 學, 学, xué =hsüeh, study	学 学 学 学 学 学 学 学
六 六, liù, six	六 六 六 六
算 算, suàn, calculate	算 算 算 算 算 算 算 算 算 算
五 五, wǔ, five	五 五 五 五

7. MONEY & PARTYING

得 得, dé, get 得得得得得得得得得得得

身 贝, bèi, shellfish; used as money 贝贝贝贝

朋 朋, péng =p'eng, friend 朋朋朋朋朋朋朋朋

買 买, mǎi, buy 买买买买买买

网 网, wǎng, net 网网网网网网

價 价, jià, price 价价价价价价价

金 金, jīn, gold; metal 金金金金金金金金金

錢 钱, qián = Ch'ien, money 钱钱钱钱钱钱钱钱钱

聲 声, shēng, sound 声声声声声声声

石 石, shí, stone 石石石石石

舞 舞, wǔ, dance 舞舞舞舞舞舞舞舞舞舞舞

8. WAR

兵, bīng, arms 兵兵兵兵兵兵兵

斤, jīn, a unit of weight 斤斤斤斤

新, xīn =hsin, new 新新新新新新新新新

木, mù, tree 木木木木

師, 师, shī =shih, teacher 师师师师师师

還, 还, huán; hái, return; still 还还还还还还

我, wǒ, I; me 我我我我我我

義, 义, yì, righteousness 义义义

正, zhèng, correct 正正正正正

是, shì, be; right 是是是是是是是是

旅, lǚ, travel 旅旅旅旅旅旅旅旅

從, 从, cóng =ts'ung, follow 从从从从

馬, 马, mǎ, horse 马马马

車, 车, chē, vehicle 车车车车

中, zhōng, center 中中中中

197

鼓 鼓, gǔ, drum, rouse 鼓鼓鼓鼓鼓鼓鼓鼓鼓鼓

支 支, zhī =chih, support 支支支支

至 至, zhì =chih, to; till 至至至至至至

引 引, yǐn, draw 引引引引

的 的, de, dì, target 的的的的的的的的

白 白, bái, white 白白白白白

武 武, wǔ, military 武武武武武武武武

亡 亡, wáng, flee; lose 亡亡亡

刀 刀, dāo, sword 刀刀

敗 敗, bài, defeat 敗敗敗敗敗敗敗敗

9. DEATH

免, miǎn =mien, exempt 免免免免免免免

晚 wǎn, evening; late 晚晚晚晚晚晚晚晚晚晚

病, bìng, disease; sickness 病病病病病病病病病病

老, lǎo, old 老老老老老老老

死, sǐ =ssu, death 死死死死死死死

骨, gǔ, bone 骨骨骨骨骨骨骨骨骨骨

Writing Exercise - Part 3

地 DI, EARTH

1. FROM WATER TO WATER

氣, 气, qì =ch'i, gas; air 气气气气

米, mǐ, rice 米米米米米米

泉, quán =ch'üan, spring 泉泉泉泉泉泉泉泉泉

永, yǒng, forever 永永永永永

泳, yǒng, swim 泳泳泳泳泳泳泳泳

雨, yǔ =yú, rain 雨雨雨雨雨雨雨雨

雲, 云, yún =yǔn, cloud 云云云云

205

2. FARM

畎界, jiè, boundary 界界界界界界界界界

爪介, jiè, be situated between 介介介介介

井井, jǐng, well 井井井井

3. Fun Chinese With Animals

角 角, jiǎo, horn 角角角角角角角角	
解 解, jie, separate 解解解解解解解解解解解	
爲 爲, 为, wèi, support; do 为为为为	
象 象, xiàng =hsiang, elephant 象象象象象象象象象象	
狂 狂, kuáng, mad 狂狂狂狂狂狂	
龍 龍, 龙, lóng, dragon 龙龙龙龙龙	
舊 舊, 旧, jiù, past 旧旧旧旧旧旧	
觀 觀, 观, guàn, observe 观观观观观观	
鳥 鳥, 鸟, niǎo, bird 鸟鸟鸟鸟鸟	
蟲 蟲, 虫, chóng, insect 虫虫虫虫虫虫	
强 强, qiáng, strong 强强强强强强强强强强	
風 風, 风, fēng, wind 风风风风	
萬 萬, 万, wàn, ten thousand 万万万	
九 九, jiǔ, nine 九九	

209

4. HUNTING

單 單, 单, dān, single 单单单单单单单单单

離 離, 离, lí, leave 离离离离离离离离离

魚 魚, 鱼, yú =yü, fish 鱼鱼鱼鱼鱼鱼鱼鱼

小 小, xiǎo =hsiao, small 小小小

豊 豐, 丰, fēng, abundant 丰丰丰丰

豆 豆, dòu, bean 豆豆豆豆豆豆豆豆

禮 禮, 礼, lǐ, ceremony; courtesy 礼礼礼礼礼礼

來 來, 来, lái, come 来来来来来来来来

麥 麥, 麦, mài, wheat; barley 麦麦麦麦麦麦麦麦

600 Basic Chinese Words

HSK(3rd Grade)

1	阿姨	āyí	auntie
2	啊	a	huh
3	矮	ǎi	short
4	爱	ài	love
5	爱好	àihào	be keen on
6	安静	ānjìng	quiet
7	八	bā	eight
8	把	bǎ	hold
9	爸爸	bàba	dad
10	吧	ba	let's…
11	白	bái	white
12	百	bǎi	hundred
13	班	bān	class
14	搬	bān	take … away
15	半	bàn	half
16	办法	bànfǎ	way
17	办公室	bàngōngshì	office
18	帮忙	bāngmáng	help
19	帮助	bāngzhù	help
20	包	bāo	wrap

21	饱	bǎo	full
22	报纸	bàozhǐ	newspaper
23	杯子	bēizi	cup
24	北方	běifāng	north
25	北京	Běijīng	Beijing
26	被	bèi	quilt
27	本	běn	root; basis
28	鼻子	bízi	nose
29	比	bǐ	compare
30	比较	bǐjiào	relatively
31	比赛	bǐsài	match
32	必须	bìxū	must
33	变化	biànhuà	change
34	表示	biǎoshì	express
35	表演	biǎoyǎn	perform
36	别	bié	other
37	别人	biéren	other people
38	宾馆	bīnguǎn	hotel
39	冰箱	bīngxiāng	refrigerator
40	不 客气	bú kèqi	You're welcome.
41	不	bù	not
42	才	cái	ability
43	菜	cài	vegetable
44	菜单	càidān	menu
45	参加	cānjiā	take part in
46	草	cǎo	grass
47	层	céng	floor
48	茶	chá	tea
49	差	chà	difference
50	长	cháng	long
51	唱歌	chànggē	sing
52	超市	chāoshì	supermarket
53	衬衫	chènshān	shirt
54	成绩	chéngjì	success
55	城市	chéngshì	city
56	吃	chī	eat
57	迟到	chídào	be late

58	出	chū	go out
59	出现	chūxiàn	to appear
60	出租车	chūzūchē	taxi
61	厨房	chúfáng	kitchen
62	除了	chúle	except
63	穿	chuān	wear
64	船	chuán	boat
65	春	chūn	spring
66	词语	cíyǔ	term
67	次	cì	time
68	聪明	cōngming	clever
69	从	cóng	follow
70	错	cuò	incorrect
71	打电话	dǎ diànhuà	make a telephone call
72	打篮球	dǎ lánqiú	to play basketball
73	打扫	dǎsǎo	clean
74	打算	dǎsuàn	plan
75	大	dà	big
76	大家	dàjiā	master
77	带	dài	take
78	担心	dānxīn	worry
79	蛋糕	dàngāo	cake
80	但是	dànshì	but
81	当然	dāngrán	of course
82	到	dào	arrive
83	地	dì	the Earth
84	的	de	aux. (~' s)
85	得	de	aux. (capability or possibility)
86	灯	dēng	light
87	等	děng	grade; wait
88	低	dī	low
89	弟弟	dìdi	younger brother
90	地方	dìfang	place
91	地铁	dìtiě	Subway
92	地图	dìtú	map
93	第一	dì-yī	first
94	点	diǎn	o' clock

95	电脑	diànnǎo	computer
96	电视	diànshì	television
97	电梯	diàntī	elevator
98	电影	diànyǐng	movie
99	电子邮件	diànzǐ yóujiàn	e-mail
100	东	dōng	east
101	东西	dōngxi	thing
102	冬	dōng	winter
103	懂	dǒng	understand
104	动物	dòngwù	animal
105	都	dōu	all
106	读	dú	read
107	短	duǎn	short
108	段	duàn	period
109	锻炼	duànliàn	work out
110	对	duì	answer (yes)
111	对不起	duìbuqǐ	be sorry
112	多	duō	a lot of
113	多么	duōme	how
114	多少	duōshao	how many
115	饿	è	hungry
116	而且	érqiě	and what's more
117	儿子	érzi	son
118	耳朵	ěrduo	ear
119	二	èr	two
120	发烧	fāshāo	have a temperature
121	发现	fāxiàn	discover
122	饭馆	fànguǎn	restaurant
123	方便	fāngbiàn	convenient
124	房间	fángjiān	room
125	放	fàng	release
126	放心	fàngxīn	set one's mind at rest
127	非常	fēicháng	very
128	飞机	fēijī	airplane
129	分	fēn	divide;minute
130	分钟	fēnzhōng	minute;min.
131	服务员	fúwùyuán	attendant

132	附近	fùjìn	nearby
133	复习	fùxí	revise
134	干净	gānjìng	clean
135	敢	gǎn	dare
136	感冒	gǎnmào	catch a cold
137	刚才	gāngcái	just now
138	高	gāo	tall;high
139	高兴	gāoxìng	happy
140	告诉	gàosu	tell
141	哥哥	gēge	elder brother
142	个	gè	individual
143	给	gěi	provide
144	跟	gēn	heel;with
145	根据	gēnjù	according to
146	更	gèng	even more
147	公共汽车	gōnggòngqìchē	bus
148	公斤	gōngjīn	kilogram
149	公司	gōngsī	company
150	公园	gōngyuán	Park
151	工作	gōngzuò	work
152	狗	gǒu	dog
153	故事	gùshi	story
154	刮 风	guā fēng	blow
155	关	guān	close
156	关系	guānxì	relation
157	关心	guānxīn	be concerned
158	关于	guānyú	With Reference to
159	贵	guì	expensive
160	国家	guójiā	state
161	果汁	guǒzhī	Juice
162	过去	guòqù	the past
163	过	guo	pass through
164	还	hái	still, yet
165	还是	háishì	still, or
166	孩子	háizi	child
167	害怕	hàipà	be afraid
168	汉语	Hànyǔ	Chinese

169	好	hǎo	good
170	好吃	hǎochī	Good taste
171	号	hào	number
172	喝	hē	drink
173	和	hé	and
174	河	hé	river
175	黑	hēi	black
176	黑板	hēibǎn	blackboard
177	很	hěn	very
178	红	hóng	red
179	后面	hòumiàn	back
180	护照	hùzhào	passport
181	花	huā	flower;spend
182	花园	huāyuán	Garden
183	画	huà	draw
184	坏	huài	bad
185	欢迎	huānyíng	welcome
186	还	huán	return
187	环境	huánjìng	environment
188	换	huàn	exchange
189	黄	huáng	yellow
190	回	huí	return
191	回答	huídá	answer
192	会	huì	be able to
193	会议	huìyì	meeting
194	火车站	huǒchēzhàn	train station
195	或者	huòzhě	maybe
196	机场	jīchǎng	airport
197	鸡蛋	jīdàn	egg
198	几乎	jīhū	almost
199	机会	jīhuì	opportunity
200	极	jí	extreme
201	几	jǐ	how many; a few
202	记得	jìde	remember
203	季节	jìjié	season
204	家	jiā	family
205	检查	jiǎnchá	examine

206	简单	jiǎndān	simple
207	件	jiàn	item
208	健康	jiànkāng	healthy
209	见面	jiànmiàn	meet
210	讲	jiǎng	speak
211	教	jiāo	teach
212	角	jiǎo	horn;angle
213	脚	jiǎo	foot
214	叫	jiào	call
215	教室	jiàoshì	classroom
216	接	jiē	draw near;connect
217	街道	jiēdào	street
218	结婚	jiéhūn	get married
219	结束	jiéshù	end
220	节目	jiémù	program
221	节日	jiérì	festival
222	姐姐	jiějie	elder sister
223	解决	jiějué	resolve
224	借	jiè	borrow
225	介绍	jièshào	introduce
226	今天	jīntiān	today
227	进	jìn	advance
228	近	jìn	near
229	经常	jīngcháng	often
230	经过	jīngguò	pass
231	经理	jīnglǐ	manager
232	九	jiǔ	nine
233	久	jiǔ	long
234	旧	jiù	old;used
235	就	jiù	then
236	举行	jǔxíng	hold
237	句子	jùzi	sentence
238	觉得	juéde	feel;think
239	决定	juédìng	decide
240	咖啡	kāfēi	coffee
241	开	kāi	open
242	开始	kāishǐ	start, begin

243	看	kàn	look at
244	看见	kànjiàn	see
245	考试	kǎoshì	sit an exam
246	渴	kě	thirsty
247	可爱	kě'ài	adorable;cute
248	可能	kěnéng	maybe
249	可以	kěyǐ	can
250	刻	kè	engrave
251	课	kè	subject;class
252	客人	kèrén	guest
253	空调	kōngtiáo	air conditioner
254	口	kǒu	mouth
255	哭	kū	cry
256	裤子	kùzi	trousers
257	块	kuài	lump
258	快	kuài	fast;quick
259	快乐	kuàilè	happy
260	筷子	kuàizi	chopsticks
261	来	lái	come
262	蓝	lán	blue
263	老	lǎo	old
264	老师	lǎoshī	teacher
265	了	le	finish/ complete
266	累	lèi	tired
267	冷	lěng	cold
268	离	lí	from
269	离开	líkāi	leave
270	里	lǐ	inside
271	礼物	lǐwù	present
272	历史	lìshǐ	history
273	脸	liǎn	face
274	练习	liànxí	practice
275	两	liǎng	two
276	辆	liàng	measure word (cars)
277	了解	liǎojiě	understand
278	邻居	línjū	neighbour
279	零	líng	zero

280	六	liù	six
281	楼	lóu	tall building; floor
282	路	lù	road
283	旅游	lǚyóu	tour
284	绿	lù	green
285	妈妈	māma	mom
286	马	mǎ	horse
287	马上	mǎshàng	right away
288	吗	ma	(used at the end of the question)
289	买	mǎi	buy
290	卖	mài	sell
291	满意	mǎnyì	be satisfied
292	慢	màn	slow
293	忙	máng	busy
294	猫	māo	cat
295	帽子	màozi	hat
296	没	méi	not have
297	没关系	méi guānxi	It doesn't matter.
298	每	měi	every
299	妹妹	mèimei	every, each
300	门	mén	door
301	米	mǐ	rice;meter
302	米饭	mǐfàn	cooked rice
303	面包	miànbāo	bread
304	面条	miàntiáo	noodle
305	明白	míngbai	understand
306	明天	míngtiān	tomorrow
307	名字	míngzi	name
308	拿	ná	hold
309	哪（哪儿）	nǎ (nǎr)	which (where)
310	那（那儿）	nà (nàr)	that (there)
311	奶奶	nǎinai	grandmother
312	南	nán	south
313	男人	nánrén	man
314	难	nán	difficult
315	难过	nánguò	have a hard time
316	呢	ne	(used for emphasis in a question)

317	能	néng	can
318	你	nǐ	you
319	年	nián	year
320	年级	niánjí	grade
321	年轻	niánqīng	young
322	鸟	niǎo	bird
323	您	nín	you (to elders)
324	牛奶	niúnǎi	milk
325	努力	nǔlì	try hard
326	女儿	nǚ'ér	daughter
327	女人	nǚrén	woman
328	爬山	páshān	go climbing
329	盘子	pánzi	plate
330	旁边	pángbiān	side
331	胖	pàng	fat
332	跑步	pǎobù	run
333	朋友	péngyou	friend
334	啤酒	píjiǔ	beear
335	便宜	piányi	cheap
336	票	piào	ticket
337	漂亮	piàoliang	good-looking
338	苹果	píngguǒ	apple
339	葡萄	pútao	grape
340	普通话	pǔtōnghuà	mandarin
341	七	qī	seven
342	妻子	qīzi	wife
343	其实	qíshí	actually
344	其他	qítā	other
345	骑	qí	ride
346	奇怪	qíguài	strange
347	起床	qǐchuáng	get up
348	千	qiān	thousand
349	铅笔	qiānbǐ	pensil
350	钱	qián	money
351	前面	qiánmiàn	frond
352	清楚	qīngchu	clear
353	晴	qíng	fine (weather)

354	请	qǐng	please
355	秋	qiū	fall
356	去	qù	go
357	去年	qùnián	last year
358	裙子	qúnzi	skirt
359	然后	ránhòu	afterwards
360	让	ràng	let
361	热	rè	hot
362	热情	rèqíng	passion
363	人	rén	human being
364	认识	rènshi	know
365	认为	rènwéi	think
366	认真	rènzhēn	serious
367	日	rì	sun;day
368	容易	róngyì	easy
369	如果	rúguǒ	if
370	三	sān	three
371	伞	sǎn	umbrella
372	商店	shāngdiàn	store
373	上	shàng	up;go
374	上班	shàngbān	go to work
375	上网	shàngwǎng	go online
376	上午	shàngwǔ	morning
377	少	shǎo	few
378	谁	shéi	who
379	身体	shēntǐ	body
380	什么	shénme	what
381	生病	shēngbìng	fall ill; get sick
382	生气	shēngqì	angry
383	生日	shēngrì	birthday
384	声音	shēngyīn	sound
385	十	shí	ten
386	时候	shíhou	time
387	时间	shíjiān	time
388	使	shǐ	use;let
389	是	shì	beear
390	世界	shìjiè	world

391	事情	shìqing	matter
392	手表	shǒubiǎo	watch
393	手机	shǒujī	mobile phone
394	瘦	shòu	thin
395	书	shū	book
396	舒服	shūfu	comfortable
397	叔叔	shūshu	uncle
398	树	shù	tree
399	数学	shùxué	mathematics
400	刷 牙	shuā yá	brush one's teeth
401	双	shuāng	two
402	水	shuǐ	water
403	水果	shuǐguǒ	fruit
404	水平	shuǐpíng	level
405	睡觉	shuìjiào	sleep
406	说话	shuōhuà	talk
407	司机	sījī	driver
408	四	sì	four
409	送	sòng	send
410	虽然	suīrán	although
411	岁	suì	year (counting age)
412	所以	suǒyǐ	so
413	他	tā	he
414	她	tā	she
415	它	tā	it
416	太	tài	too
417	太阳	tàiyáng	sun
418	糖	táng	sugar
419	特别	tèbié	peculiar
420	疼	téng	winter
421	踢 足球	tī zúqiú	to play soccer
422	题	tí	subject
423	提高	tígāo	raise
424	体育	tǐyù	sport
425	天气	tiānqì	weather
426	甜	tián	sweet
427	条	tiáo	twig

428	跳舞	tiàowǔ	dance
429	听	tīng	listen
430	同事	tóngshì	colleague
431	同学	tóngxué	fellow student
432	同意	tóngyì	agree
433	头发	tóufa	hair
434	突然	tūrán	suddenly
435	图书馆	túshūguǎn	library
436	腿	tuǐ	leg
437	外	wài	outside
438	完	wán	whole
439	完成	wánchéng	complete
440	玩	wán	play
441	碗	wǎn	bowl
442	晚上	wǎnshang	evening
443	万	wàn	ten thousand
444	忘记	wàngjì	forget
445	喂	wèi	hello
446	为	wèi	for
447	为了	wèile	in order to
448	为 什么	wèi shénme	why
449	位	wèi	location; digit (person)
450	文化	wénhuà	culture
451	问	wèn	ask
452	问题	wèntí	question
453	我	wǒ	I;me
454	我们	wǒmen	we
455	五	wǔ	five
456	西	xī	west
457	西瓜	xīguā	Watermelon
458	希望	xīwàng	hope
459	习惯	xíguàn	be used to, habit
460	洗	xǐ	wash
461	洗手间	xǐshǒujiān	toilets
462	洗澡	xǐzǎo	have a bath
463	喜欢	xǐhuan	like
464	下	xià	go down

465	下午	xiàwǔ	afternoon
466	下雨	xià yǔ	rain
467	夏	xià	summer
468	先	xiān	earlier
469	先生	xiānsheng	Mr.
470	现在	xiànzài	now
471	香蕉	xiāngjiāo	banana
472	相同	xiāngtóng	identical
473	相信	xiāngxìn	believe
474	想	xiǎng	think
475	向	xiàng	direction;to
476	像	xiàng	look like
477	小	xiǎo	small
478	小姐	xiǎojiě	Miss
479	小时	xiǎoshí	hour
480	小心	xiǎoxīn	be careful
481	笑	xiào	laugh
482	校长	xiàozhǎng	principal
483	些	xiē	some
484	鞋	xié	shoe
485	写	xiě	write
486	谢谢	xièxie	thank you
487	新	xīn	new
488	新闻	xīnwén	news
489	新鲜	xīnxiān	fresh
490	信	xìn	believe;character
491	星期	xīngqī	week
492	行李箱	xínglixiāng	bag; case
493	姓	xìng	surname
494	兴趣	xìngqù	interest
495	熊猫	xióngmāo	panda
496	休息	xiūxi	rest
497	需要	xūyào	need
498	选择	xuǎnzé	choose
499	学生	xuésheng	student
500	学习	xuéxí	study
501	学校	xuéxiào	school

502	雪	xuě	snow
503	颜色	yánsè	color
504	眼镜	yǎnjìng	eyeglasses
505	眼睛	yǎnjing	eye
506	羊肉	yángròu	mutton
507	要求	yāoqiú	demand
508	药	yào	medicine
509	要	yào	will
510	爷爷	yéye	granddad
511	也	yě	also
512	一	yī	one
513	衣服	yīfu	clothes
514	医生	yīshēng	doctor
515	医院	yīyuàn	hospital
516	一定	yídìng	definitely
517	一共	yígòng	altogether
518	一会儿	yíhuìr	a while
519	一样	yíyàng	same
520	以后	yǐhòu	after
521	以前	yǐqián	before
522	以为	yǐwéi	think
523	已经	yǐjīng	already
524	椅子	yǐzi	chair
525	一般	yìbān	ordinary
526	一边	yìbiān	side
527	一起	yìqǐ	together
528	一直	yìzhí	straight
529	意思	yìsi	meaning
530	阴	yīn	overcast
531	因为	yīnwèi	because
532	音乐	yīnyuè	music
533	银行	yínháng	bank
534	应该	yīnggāi	should
535	影响	yǐngxiǎng	affect
536	用	yòng	use
537	游戏	yóuxì	game
538	游泳	yóuyǒng	swim

539	有	yǒu	have
540	有名	yǒumíng	famous
541	又	yòu	again
542	右边	yòubian	right
543	鱼	yú	fish
544	遇到	yùdào	encounter
545	元	yuán	first;yuan
546	远	yuǎn	far
547	愿意	yuànyì	be willing to
548	月	yuè	month
549	月亮	yuèliang	the moon
550	越	yuè	jump over
551	云	yún	cloud
552	运动	yùndòng	sport
553	在	zài	be
554	再	zài	again
555	再见	zàijiàn	say goodbye
556	早上	zǎoshang	morning
557	怎么	zěnme	how
558	怎么样	zěnmeyàng	how2
559	站	zhàn	stand
560	张	zhāng	open
561	长	zhǎng	older, head
562	丈夫	zhàngfu	husband
563	着急	zháojí	worried
564	找	zhǎo	look for
565	照顾	zhàogù	look after
566	照片	zhàopiàn	photograph
567	照相机	zhàoxiàngjī	camera
568	这（这儿）	zhè（zhèr）	this（here）
569	着	zhe	~ing;touch
570	真	zhēn	true;really
571	正在	zhèngzài	right now
572	知道	zhīdào	know
573	只	zhǐ	only
574	中国	Zhōngguó	China
575	中间	zhōngjiān	middle

576	中午	zhōngwǔ	noon
577	终于	zhōngyú	finally
578	种	zhǒng	species
579	重要	zhòngyào	important
580	周末	zhōumò	weekend
581	主要	zhǔyào	major
582	住	zhù	live
583	祝	zhù	wish
584	注意	zhùyì	be careful
585	准备	zhǔnbèi	prepare
586	桌子	zhuōzi	table
587	字	zì	character
588	字典	zìdiǎn	dictionary
589	自己	zìjǐ	oneself
590	自行车	zǒngshì	bicycle
591	总是	zǒngshì	always
592	走	zǒu	walk
593	最	zuì	most
594	最近	zuìjìn	recent
595	昨天	zuótiān	yesterday
596	左边	zuǒbian	left
597	坐	zuò	sit
598	做	zuò	make
599	作业	zuòyè	work
600	作用	zuòyòng	affect

Printed in the United States
By Bookmasters